KASSEM EID is a Palestinian–Syrian rebel and human rights activist. In 2014 he went on a speaking tour across the United States and testified before the United Nations Security Council. He has contributed to the *New York Times, Washington Post* and the *Wall Street Journal*, and s interviewed on *60 Minutes*. He is currently a refugee g in Germany.

My Country

KASSEM EID

BLOOMSBURY PUBLISHING

LONDON · OXFORD · NEW YORK · NEW DELHI · SYDNEY

BLOOMSBURY PUBLISHING
Bloomsbury Publishing Plc
50 Bedford Square, London, WC1B 3DP, UK

BLOOMSBURY, BLOOMSBURY PUBLISHING and the
Diana logo are trademarks of Bloomsbury Publishing Plc

First published in Great Britain 2018
This edition published 2019

A catalogue record for this book is available from the British Library.

ISBN: PB: 978-1-4088-9513-9; EBOOK: 978-1-4088-9511-5

2 4 6 8 10 9 7 5 3 1

Typeset by Integra Software Services Pvt. Ltd.
Printed and bound in Great Britain by CPI Group (UK) Ltd,
Croydon CR0 4YY

MIX
Paper from
responsible sources
FSC® C020471

To find out more about our authors and books visit www.bloomsbury.com
and sign up for our newsletters

I'm grateful for your love, kindness, courage and strength. I wrote it for you.

Foreword

In the early pre-dawn of 21 August 2013, at a time of the year when many people were vacationing and trying hard not to read the newspapers or listen to news on the radio or television, rockets containing the chemical agent sarin landed on the opposition-controlled areas of Damascus known as the Ghouta agricultural belt.

As a result of those attacks, an estimated 1,429 people died, many of them children. UN Secretary General Ban Ki-moon – who had been characteristically passive on other events of the Syrian war – said the attack constituted a war crime and went as far as to call it the 'most significant confirmed use of chemical weapons against civilians since Saddam Hussein used them' in Halabja, against the Kurds, in 1988.

Death by sarin is one of the most horrific ways to die, if one can be so crass as to rank ways to die, especially during wartime. When the chemical creeps into your system, you choke, you cannot breathe, you suffocate. You vomit. Death is excruciating, slow and vicious. Dying, you might wonder who could do this to another human being – and why.

How does the landscape of war become a cemetery? How does this happen to ordinary people? *My Country*

tells this story. Many years ago Ghouta was an oasis near
the Barada River, a farming district where fruit trees flour-
ished, before the urban sprawl of Damascus swallowed
it. Once, 80,000 people lived in Moadamiya, where the
author, Kassem Eid, grew up; by the time of the sarin
attack, which came two years into the war between
President Bashar al-Assad and his forces and the Syrian
opposition, there were only 10,000. These were the
unlucky ones who had not managed to flee. The ones who
were left were trapped by a medieval siege and they were
slowly starving to death. Many were reduced to eating
weeds and leaves. Children roamed the streets looking for
food, for solace.

During the war Ghouta became synonymous with
resistance to President Bashar al-Assad. Its people, as
Kassem Eid explains, first protested with street marches
and demonstrations, and later took up arms to protect
themselves and their land. For this they were gassed by
their own government.

One of the survivors of the attack was someone who
had grown up reading old battered copies of *Reader's
Digest* to learn English, who liked to play video games,
who adored his parents and his siblings, and who had
dreams of living in a country where he could be truly free.
That man was Kassem Eid, a young man who worked
with journalists and media groups as a translator. On the
morning of the attack Kassem was living in an abandoned
apartment with some friends. Like the other residents
of Moadamiya, he was also starving to death – reduced
to scrounging through the garbage and rubble, grateful
when he found weeds to make soup. But the fierce pain
of hunger was the least of his problems once the attack
started.

Kassem survived the chemical attack, trying to resuscitate children turning hideous shades, he would remember, of red, yellow and blue. He saw his friends and neighbours die. The scenes he describes of that day are akin to being guided into the eighth circle of hell, Malebolge, the evil ditches, but in his case there was no Virgil, no guide. Kassem survived but has been haunted by those around him who did not. Like many survivors of wartime atrocities, he has wondered why he was spared and others were not.

Later that day he followed fighters of the Free Syrian Army to the front line. He had not fought before – he was just a kid – but what he had seen changed him. Shortly after the attack he fired his first bullet. He described this as an act of defence, on behalf of the land that had been 'poisoned by his enemies'.

This is the story of what happens to one man who grows up believing life will go one way and then sees it shift, horribly, irrevocably, in another direction – because of war. It is also about survival and resilience. It is about living through the worst conditions imaginable, escaping and starting again.

My Country is Kassem's book of memory, and it gives us a window into growing up in the Syria of the 1980s and 90s, a closed country ruled by a dictatorship. It is a story of life in Assad's Syria as a Sunni Muslim but also as a Palestinian, a minority in a country of minorities. It is the story of having dreams that are crushed, but remaining undefeated.

It is nearly eight years since the war in Syria began. Eight years of misery is unfathomable. Think about it in terms of a single human life. It's the time it takes an infant to sit up, learn to walk, tie their shoes, learn to read and write and enter what the French call the age of reason. Eight years is for ever. A tree can grow more than three metres in eight years.

For a war to run that long, it means that societies will have to shift and change drastically. It means that families, like Kassem's, will be torn apart, that diplomas that were meant to be will never be obtained, that love stories that might have been will never be. Too many children die. Too many people suffer in ways we cannot imagine. War destroys the landscape, interior and exterior, of every human being it touches.

But eight years also means people cease to listen and to extend their natural empathy, which is why this book is so important. Even if the war in Syria ends tomorrow, what has been born from it will live for years to come. War does not end with a ceasefire and a treaty; it continues in the children and their children not yet born, who grow up with the cycle of violence. The 1992–6 siege of Sarajevo, for instance, the longest siege of a capital city in modern history, lasted less than half as long as what Syria is now enduring, yet the repercussions of that battle will be felt for generations. And by the time the Bosnian War ended, the world had long ago turned off its television sets. We cannot afford to do that with Syria. We must pay attention to what is happening in that region, because it will in many ways come back to affect us.

This book is a powerful indictment of humanity, but it is also a book about its survival. The individual is much more resilient than we imagine. This is a story of love and death but also of hope.

                                        Janine di Giovanni

Contents

SYRIA

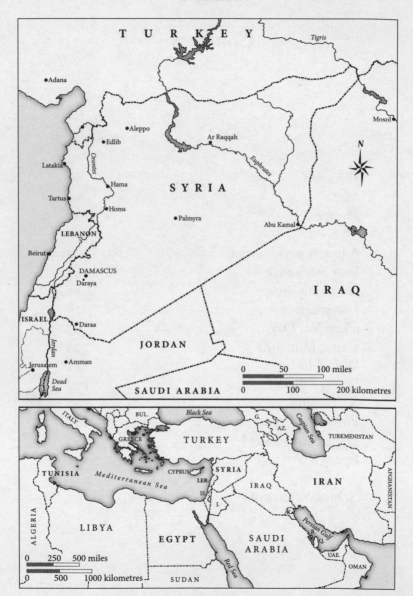

MOADAMIYA

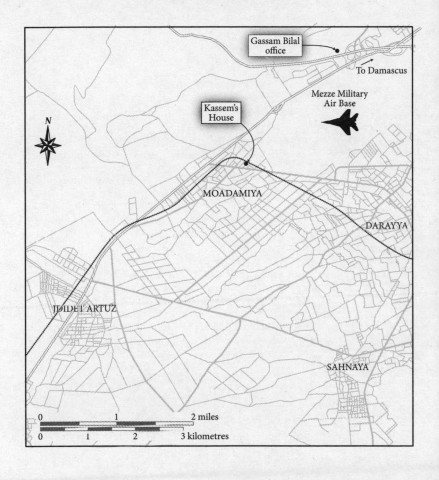

Preface

I came to Germany a broken man.

I tried to pray like I used to, in the hope that I would find peace, but I did not. I started drinking again, smoking and dancing like crazy at nightclubs, but I could not distract myself. I exercised to the point of exhaustion to try to cool the burning fire inside me, but this only made the flames glow brighter.

I can never forget. The joyful laughter of my friends still rings in my ears like ancient love songs, jolting me awake at night and stopping me dead in the middle of the day. When I hear these siren songs, I am pulled back towards the abyss, towards my beloved Syria and my childhood home, from which I barely escaped. I am overcome by sadness and shame at my failure to save my friends.

I am terribly confused. I can't stop thinking about Syria, I can't forget all that I've been through, and, above all, I can't believe that humanity has become so deaf and blind to the thousands of Syrians with stories like mine. I was lucky enough to live to tell this tale, while so many others struggled, fought and died silently.

I have written this memoir for them. I hope that it will give a voice to those who are suffering now, and to those who have been silenced for ever – and that people of conscience around the world will listen, before it is too late.

A lesson well learned
1989–2002

My family moved to Moadamiya when I was just three years old. It was the summer of 1989. I sat on the back of the moving truck next to my brother Mishael as we bumped and jolted our way down the unpaved road. We were kids and thought that moving was an exciting adventure; we shouted and sang throughout the drive, and we exploded in laughter every time the truck hit a bump.

We were leaving our old house in the Qadam neighbourhood in the Syrian capital of Damascus, where I was born. I was the eighth child of a typically large Palestinian-Syrian family. My oldest brother Yazid was almost fourteen; after him came my brothers Razwan, Yeman and Raylan, then my sister Gazwa, then two more brothers, Bara and Mishael – then me. When we moved, my youngest brother Muhammad was still nursing, and Waddah and Ahmad were not yet born.

My father, Fawaz, was an editor at Syrian National TV, while my mother, Selwa, stayed at home and looked after us. Both my parents' families were originally from Palestine. My father had four brothers and six sisters, and my mother had five brothers and two sisters – like I said,

typically large. Although both families had owned pros-
perous farms, they were forced to flee when the Israelis
took over parts of Palestine in the 1948 war, an event
known to Palestinians as the *Nakba* – the catastrophe. My
father's family walked north until they reached the Syrian
border, while my mother's family headed east to Jordan,
which is where she was born. Both families arrived in
their new countries with nothing.

Because she was born in Jordan, my mother was a
Jordanian citizen, but my father's situation was far more
difficult. He was born in a small town called Samakh, at
the southern end of Lake Tiberius in the north of Palestine,
and he was about twelve when the *Nakba* occurred.
Palestinians are considered 'guests', not full citizens in
Syria. The authorities believe that, should there be a chance
to go back to their home country, Palestinians will take it.
This sounds reasonable in principle, but in reality it means
Palestinians living in Syria could never fully integrate into
society, and remained refugees, without the full rights of
citizens. As a result of these restrictions my father's family
struggled to make ends meet, and to help out the family
he and his brothers worked as labourers on construction
sites after school. I remember my father's hands were like
rocks, covered in scars from his time on the sites. He
would give all his earnings to his mother, but the family's
combined income often couldn't even stretch to shoes. He
told me that, when he'd finished high school and began
attending college, he'd often go to classes barefoot.

But my father was resourceful and excelled at school,
particularly in his favourite subjects, poetry and history. He
went on to the University of Damascus, where he earned a
lecturing diploma in Arabic language and literature. After
teaching for a few years in Deraa, an impoverished area of

southern Syria, he met my mother on a trip to Jordan to visit his family, who had scattered across the Middle East after the *Nakba*. She was just seventeen when they met, my father more than ten years her senior. But he had to earn her hand in marriage, so my father moved to Saudi Arabia, working long hours as a poet, writer and radio broadcaster, until he had finally raised enough money to marry her.

They lived together in Saudi Arabia for eleven years, during which time six of my older brothers were born. My father earned good money, enough to put aside as savings, which he sent back to his mother in Syria in the form of gold and jewellery and she buried in the garden for safekeeping. At the time this was seen as normal – so many people distrusted the regime and feared putting their money into government-owned banks – but in a twist of fate my grandmother developed Alzheimer's disease, and forgot where she had hidden everything. In 1982 my parents returned to Syria, so my father could help take care of his mother. Needless to say, they looked everywhere for the gold, but the search was fruitless. To this day my father's savings from his time in Saudi Arabia are buried somewhere in the earth of Syria.

The house that we left behind in Damascus in 1989 was like a villa – it had seven rooms, a fountain and a large courtyard. Grape vines adorned the walls of the outdoor space, with blackberry bushes nestling beneath and apple trees dotted around. My mother loved tending the garden, but the house was in what was considered a dangerous neighbourhood – at that time there was a train station very close by, with a decrepit old train that occasionally went to two or three Syrian cities, but was almost

defunct. The area had become known for drugs, prostitution, fights. The houses were also built very close together,
so close that you could jump from one to another. One
day, after my mother had hung up the washing on our
rooftop, somebody sneaked over our wall and stole the
half-dry clothes. But the final straw came when thieves
tried to break into the house while we were sleeping – my
dad and brothers went up to the roof one morning to
find the doors kicked in. My mother became too scared
to stay. She promised us that, while our new house would
be smaller, our new neighbourhood would be much safer,
and we could lead a happier life.

Moadamiya, only three miles from Damascus, felt like a
different world. Instead of boring, hulking city buildings,
there were old mud houses that looked like something
from the fairy tales my mother read us at bedtime. The
air was fresh and crisp, and the town was surrounded by
fields of flowers and olive groves. As we arrived, I even saw
two children racing down the road on horseback. Our
new home was on the top floor of one of the few modern
buildings: a three-storey, communist-style apartment
complex built by the Ministry of Media for its employees.
We had two large bedrooms and a living room, and two
balconies, one facing east, one west. There was a small
kitchen and a tiny bathroom.

Our neighbours were simple, loving people. Most of
them had been born in this small town, their parents
and grandparents before them, farming the olive groves
through generations. On our first day, two offered to
help us move in. More neighbours soon visited, bringing
gifts of olives and olive oil. Three families lived across the
street: those of Abu Khaled and his wife Um Khaled, Abu
and Um Ummar, and Abu and Um Ali. (Syrian couples

like to take on the nicknames Abu and Um – Father and Mother – followed by the name of their first child.)

My parents quickly became good friends with our neighbours. Mama in particular would spend time each day sitting with the rest of the women discussing food, cooking and the best bargains at the local market. The women taught Mama which produce to buy at which time, and how to preserve food – things she hadn't needed to know in the city. They also taught her how to make apricot jam and *maqdous*, a Syrian dish of aubergines, nuts and red chilli peppers. Because my family was so large, Mama's friends would help her to prepare massive quantities of jam, *maqdous* and boiled vegetables to use and store over long periods.

Like most country folk in Syria, the families on my street each had at least five children. Syrians in the countryside tend to have large families because they depend on farming to live; in the cities families are a bit smaller, normally around three to four children. But Palestinians in Syria have the highest number of children per family, and we were no different. Growing up in a large family had lots of ups and downs. As a child I loved it because you never felt bored – there was always someone to talk to, play and fight with – but we had little money and it was not easy.

Because our apartment in Moadamiya had only two bedrooms, a living room, one bathroom and a kitchen, space was tight. At night we children would sleep in the big bedroom and living room, while my mother and father had a smaller room to themselves. Luckily, there was a large rooftop that only my family, and occasionally an old neighbour downstairs, would use – it was like having another room. In the summer months some of us chose to sleep outside under the stars. As we grew older, we would use the space to invite friends around, and hang out playing cards and smoking cigarettes.

Life was tough for my mother, with so many of us to look after. Not only was she cooking for twelve people, three times a day, but she was cleaning up after us too. The road outside was unpaved – only the main road was asphalt – so my poor mother struggled with all the dirt we would carry in with us, on our clothes and on ourselves. We didn't have a washing machine, so she did everything by hand – every day, washing clothes, towels, sheets.

My father was almost always working – not just at the TV station but also at a radio station, and as a journalist, to make ends meet. He would work fifteen- or sixteen-hour days, sometimes all through the night. But on Friday (the main weekend day in Syria) he would sometimes find time to take us to our neighbours' farms out in west Moadamiya. This was perhaps my favourite thing. The roadsides were lined with stately olive trees, and I loved to look at the farm animals as we drove past. When we arrived, we would climb the fruit trees and stuff ourselves with the apricots, figs and apples that grew in abundance.

The farms were a special place for the grown-ups too. While we played, they sat together on the grass sipping tea and discussing current affairs, the situations in Israel, Palestine, America – virtually every country in the world – and they would do it in loud voices, not like at home, where they only discussed these topics quietly when they thought we couldn't hear. The only country they didn't discuss was Syria. I remember finding that strange. Why would you talk about every country in the world except for the one that you were living in?

Even though I was only a child, I could sense that the family was struggling. Our friends had better toys and more pocket money than we did. Eid parties at my friends' houses were larger and more lavish than at my family's. When our birthdays came round, my friends seemed to receive nicer clothes as presents. I couldn't quite understand why this was the case, but I knew how hard my father worked and how much he loved us.

My father did give me something that none of the other boys had. When he was living in Saudi Arabia, he had been an avid reader of *Reader's Digest*, and he had subscribed to the magazine in both English and Arabic. He brought eleven years' worth of copies back with him to Syria, although he had to smuggle them in, because it was banned. It would become the most important thing in my life, and the best gift a parent could give: the pathway to read, write and speak in English.

As a small child, going into the street to play with a ball only interested me for an hour or so, and then I would get bored. Because my older brothers and sister were attending school, our living room felt at times like a public library, as everyone returned home after class to continue studying. There was always a book open, and pencils and paper lying around. I would sit next to my siblings and look over their shoulders as they scratched mysterious symbols on to paper. I wanted to learn the alphabet, and I begged my mother until she finally found the time to teach me. One night I saw my father reading a magazine intently. I asked him what he was so interested in, and he replied that he was reading about sailors lost at sea during the First World War. 'Baba, can I read this?' I asked. He told me I was too young, but this only made me more determined. Just like my mother and the alphabet, I pestered him for weeks to teach me to read. I was so desperate to read this thing that had brought him such joy

and curiosity, to be a part of his world. Eventually I wore
him down. Slowly, he began to teach me to read.

I found the *Reader's Digest* fascinating. Each edition
had stories about many different topics and countries
from around the world, just like the grown-up conversations my parents had on the farm. I learned about the
United States of America, which seemed to be an amazing
country, the land of the free, a land of opportunity where
anything could happen. By the time I was five, I was
already spending more time reading than playing with the
other boys. I loved stories about history and space travel,
and I had even started reading the English version.

When I turned six, it was time for me to start school.
By then I was an excellent reader and could also write
quite well. My parents pushed to have me sent straight
into the second grade. The school manager was sceptical,
but after I passed the entrance exam with ease, he was
convinced. I could barely sleep from the excitement as
school approached.

My mother woke me up on the first day of school with
her warm voice and her tender smile. When I sat down
at the kitchen table, she had a breakfast of Palestinian
bread, *za'atar* (thyme), olive oil and sweet tea waiting for
me. There was also a sandwich for me to take for lunch,
and she presented me with a freshly ironed school vest to
wear over my usual clothes. The night before, my parents
had given me a special traditional black and white school
scarf that they were both very proud of. I can still remember their faces as they placed the scarf over my neck,
beaming.

In truth, I felt a little girlie in the new school vest,
which was so long that it looked like a dress, and my older

brothers made sure I felt special on my first day by teasing me relentlessly, sniggering and pointing at my uniform. But I didn't care: it was the first day of school.

My first moments inside the school building were overwhelming. There was so much going on all around me. Boys and girls were running and playing everywhere. Two big boys got into a fight just metres away from me before an adult swooped in to break it up. As I walked down the hall, trying my best to avoid getting knocked over, I collided with a much older girl who glared at me angrily. I blushed and stammered as my face turned bright red, and she slapped me across the face before I could even apologize. Then she started calling me all sorts of names – 'Dummy! Moron!' – as the kids in the hall gathered around to join in her insults.

I felt miserable. *Slapped on the first day of school, and slapped by a girl?* I wanted to run back home, but if I told my family what had happened, my brothers would never let me live it down. I could always try and fight her, but my older brother Yazid had told me that I must never hit girls. Unsure what to do, I simply stared straight ahead and kept walking. I didn't even notice as the other students began lining up.

Suddenly I felt a whack across my rear with a stick. I yelped and turned to see who had hit me. A big, angry teacher was yelling at me: 'Line up with your class!'

This left me even more scared and confused than before. I froze in place as the teacher continued to yell at me and as the other kids stared, pointed and laughed. The teacher raised her hand as if to slap me, but another teacher interceded. She bent down, smiling, and asked me my name. She told me hers – Mrs Siham. When I told her that I was new and was in the second grade, she said gently, 'That means you are in my class. I'm so happy to have you. Please line up with the rest of your classmates over there.'

I ran across, happy that Mrs Siham would be my teacher. As I stood at the end of the line, my classmates turned to stare at me. I wasn't afraid to look back at them with determination.

After we had all lined up, the school principal walked up to the school deck, stood next to a massive Syrian flag and picked up a microphone.

'Atten-tion!' she shouted, and all the kids snapped to attention. I hurried to copy them so that no one would make fun of me again.

'Salute!'

Everyone saluted.

'Arabs are one nation!'

All the kids shouted, 'Arabs are one nation!'

'Our message is immortal!'

'Our message is immortal!'

'Say it louder, stronger. Our message is immortal!'

'OUR MESSAGE IS IMMORTAL.'

'Our goals are . . .'

The children around me filled in the blank: 'Unity, freedom, socialism!'

'At ease!'

All the kids stamped at same time, making the earth shake, as they shouted, 'VANGUARDS!'

'Atten-tion!'

'*Baath!*' (Resurrection)

I didn't understand what *Baath* meant or why everyone was shouting it.

'I can't hear you, children. Louder. LOUDER!'

The children surrounding me shouted '*Baath*' over and over again, each time more loudly than the last. Something about this chant was making me uncomfortable. Eventually the principal dismissed us, and we filed off to our classrooms.

As I walked down the hall to my classroom, I looked around at the walls and lockers. They were all covered with the same words that we had just shouted. And there were other words too, in praise of 'our leader for ever, Hafez al-Assad'. I knew a little bit about Hafez al-Assad. He was the president of Syria, and I had seen his picture before – on buildings, on the sides of buses, in newspapers and in my older brothers' textbooks. And here was his picture too, plastered all over the walls of the school.

I entered the classroom. A huge photograph of Hafez al-Assad smiled down at me in greeting. I paused to stare at the picture in front of me. Hafez al-Assad was wearing a grey suit and a red tie, and he was smiling broadly. For some reason I felt afraid of the smile.

'Hey, you!' shouted a boy behind me in a strange accent. 'Why are you looking at our leader's picture like that?' I turned to look at him; he shoved me against the wall.

I hit the wall, but turned immediately and leaped on him, knocking him to the floor. The boys and girls around me stopped to watch, screaming, 'Fight! Fight!' I looked up in confusion at their shouts. The boy pushed me off him and kicked at me.

'Stop!' I heard Mrs Siham's voice. 'Get away from him, Majed! Why are you fighting? Answer me!' Neither of us answered. 'Majed, is this how you greet your new classmate on his first day of school? Apologize to Kassem right now!'

Majed turned to me and muttered, 'Sorry.' But I saw a hatred in his eyes that I had never seen before.

'Very good, Majed,' soothed Mrs Siham. 'Now, please shake Kassem's hand.'

Majed's face hardened. He stamped his feet, wheeled on Mrs Siham, and screamed, 'No!'

I looked at my teacher, expecting a harsh response. She seemed strangely nervous. I rushed to grab Majed's hand and shook it vigorously. Majed turned his angry and hate-filled stare back to me. We glared at each other for a moment, and then Mrs Siham quietly but firmly ordered Majed to take his seat.

Mrs Siham took a deep breath, cleared her throat and motioned me to the front of the class. 'Good morning, everyone,' she said. 'Welcome back to school. I'd like you to meet your new classmate, Kassem. Please join me in giving him a warm welcome.' She spoke the words 'warm welcome' directly at Majed. Mrs Siham then escorted me to the last empty seat.

The rest of the day was more like what I had expected. Mrs Siham taught us arithmetic in the morning, and I kept my hand raised for the entire class, answering most of her questions. At lunchtime I ate the olive and *za'atar* sandwich my mother had prepared. The afternoon classes went by in a blur because I was so eager to get home. I had a lot of questions to ask my parents.

When the final school bell rang, I dashed home as quickly as I could and knocked excitedly on the front door. I ran past my brother Bara, who opened the door, and rushed into the kitchen. Mama was washing her hands. When she heard my footsteps, she turned towards me and shouted, 'What's wrong? Who's knocking on the door like that?'

'It's just me, Mama,' I said. 'Nothing's wrong. I just have a lot of questions for you.'

The worry on her face melted into a smile, and she gave me a warm hug. 'So? My big boy Kassem. How was your first day of school?'

I think she soon regretted asking me. For the next thirty minutes I described every detail of my day – except of course the part where I had been slapped by a girl – and then I circled back to the morning ceremony to ask Mama what it all meant. Why was everyone shouting '*Baath*' over and over? Why were there slogans all over the walls? Why were pictures of Hafez al-Assad everywhere? Why was his smile scary?

I asked question after question, all the while talking too quickly to give her a chance to answer. She listened silently and nodded in acknowledgement as she prepared the rice and beans for dinner. When I ran out of questions, I just said, 'Tell me?'

She smiled. 'Go and change your clothes and wash your hands. Dinner is almost ready. When your baba comes home, we will talk about your questions together.' I was disappointed. How was I supposed to wait that long?

I stayed up way past my bedtime that night, sitting on the balcony and peering down the road for Baba. At around 10 or 11 p.m. his white Volkswagen finally turned into the road. Like a flash, I opened the front door and raced downstairs. Baba whipped the exhaustion off his face when he saw me and pulled me into a huge bear hug. 'Kassem! What are you doing up so late?'

'I want to talk to you about school. It confuses me a lot.'

'Oh,' he said quietly. Baba suddenly seemed a little strange, as if he himself was confused. 'Let's go upstairs and talk.'

We climbed the stairs together. Baba was completely silent. Mama smiled at us, but I saw fear behind her smile.

For the next fifteen minutes no one said a word. Baba went into the bedroom to change his clothes; Mama went to the kitchen and prepared his dinner. I fidgeted nervously on the balcony, growing more frightened with each passing minute. Finally, Baba came out and closed the balcony door firmly behind him. He sat on one of our cheap plastic chairs, lit a cigarette and clapped his hands on his knees.

'So, son. What would you like to know?'

I took a deep breath mixed with the awful-smelling smoke of his cigarette, then asked Baba every question on my mind. Why the awkward cheers and the huge pictures of Hafez al-Assad at school? Why was everyone in the family acting so scared today? Why did grown-ups never speak about politics outside the farms? And why did we never talk about the country that mattered most to us, Syria?

Baba's face grew very solemn. His first reply left me even more confused. 'Son, I want you to promise that you will never mention anything that you just told me, or anything that I am about to tell you, to anyone. Not to your teacher. Not to our neighbours. Not even to your brothers. Can you promise me that? Look me in the eyes.'

Though it was a warm summer night, I felt a chill up my spine. 'Yes, Baba.'

Baba proceeded to explain the situation in Syria to me. I didn't understand much of it then, but I soon came to an understanding of why things were the way they were, and I inherited his fears and caution. My father told me that *Baath* referred to the Baath Party, which Hafez al-Assad had hijacked after jailing, killing or exiling all his political rivals in 1970. Hafez al-Assad had built a sectarian army and police state run by people loyal only to him. He had waged a false war alongside Egyptian president Anwar al-Sadat to justify placing all Syrians under a permanent state of emergency. He had pushed Lebanon into civil war, occupied that country and ordered the massacre of innocent Lebanese and Palestinians under the guise of bringing peace. In Syria an uprising in Hama had been ended by the slaughter of an estimated 40,000 people on Assad's orders.

My father explained that he himself had avoided joining the Baath Party, even though it had cost him numerous promotion opportunities. He told me that, while he was sorry that he could not buy me all the toys and clothes that I wanted, no amount of money was worth becoming a partner in Assad's crimes. But we had to be very careful. Assad's informants were everywhere. Baba knew people who had gone missing along with their entire families simply for whispering about Hafez al-Assad. Assad could arrest or kill any Syrian he wanted. Assad could arrest us just for talking about him right now. Assad had no rules or limits. I think this is why he told me not to mention anything to my brothers, so we wouldn't talk among ourselves – it was a form of protection, and in answering my questions in this way he was trying to stop me asking them out loud, risking our family's safety.

And it worked. By this point I was thoroughly petri-fied. When Baba saw the fear on my face, he stopped and hugged me tight to his chest. Then he joked and laughed until I started laughing too, kissed me on the forehead, picked me up and carried me to bed.

Later that week I saw some kids playing football in the school yard and ran to join them. When I realized that Majed, my nemesis, was also playing, I decided that this game would have different rules. The next time Majed got the ball, I ran up to him and 'missed' the ball, kicking him in the shin. He lost control of the ball, but kicked me back before I could turn away with it. We then jabbed at the ball and at each other's legs. The ball squirted away, and we pushed and shoved each other as we sprinted after it. I noticed then that we were both smiling.

After that, during game after game, Majed and I forgot our fight on the first day of school and bonded. By the end of the first semester, he and I had become close friends. Majed then told me where his house was and invited me to visit him during the spring holidays. Conveniently, his house was located only a hundred metres from mine, in an area just past the railroad tracks called the Officers' Residence.

One day during the holidays I was playing hide-and-seek with some other boys in my neighbourhood when Majed saw me from his rooftop and whistled and waved. I was delighted when I saw that it was him and ran towards his house. My friends were yelling at me not to go, but I ignored them. I figured they were just angry with me for leaving their game.

Majed lived in a house with a tiny yard and a small garden of roses and jasmine. He was waiting for me on his doorstep when I arrived. We ran inside together. I noticed a huge picture of Hafez al-Assad in the entrance.

Majed's mother came out to greet us, wearing an apron and carrying a knife and a tomato. 'Who's here? Is this the famous Kassem? Majed has told me so much about you. Please, make yourself at home. I'll bring you some lemonade.' I was a bit shy meeting his mother for the first time, but Majed pulled me by the hand into his living room. I saw that he had an old Nintendo video game system.

'You have video games!'

'Yeah, isn't it great? My dad got them for me from Lebanon.' He gestured behind me to a picture of his father in a pilot's uniform.

'Wow! Your dad is a military pilot!'

'Do you want to play Mario or football?'

'What do you think? Football!'

We played Nintendo for the next two hours while his mum served us lemonade, cheese sandwiches and chocolate. Majed won almost every game, but I was having so much fun that I didn't even care. I only realized how late it was when the sun began to set.

Majed walked me out to the railway line and waved goodbye, and I dashed towards my house, expecting a beating from my brothers for making my mother worry, coming home so late. The front door to the apartment was cracked open, and I tried to sneak in unnoticed.

'Where do you think you're going?' My mother was sitting on a living-room chair facing me. I could tell that she was really angry. 'Where have you been?'

'I was at Majed's house.'

'Majed from your class?'

'Yeah, from my class. He lives really close – just past the railway.'

'You went past the railway?' She was yelling now.

'What did I do wrong? His mum is a teacher, his dad is a military pilot, co-pilot actually. They were very nice . . .'

Mama motioned me to silence, put her hands on my shoulders and brought her face close to mine. 'Kassem,' she said quietly, 'you are never to go past the railway line again without telling me. Understood?' It was almost more comforting when she was yelling.

I'll never forget the fear in her eyes and didn't understand it until many years later. Most of the people who lived beyond the railway were Alawites, working in the army or government. I can only think of one or two Alawite families who lived on our side. It was an unofficial border. We heard stories about people getting beaten up on the other side, or disappearing. I was eight when I heard the story of my cousin, a taxi driver, who disappeared and was never heard of again.

After the 1970 Corrective Revolution, it became clear that the Alawites separated themselves deliberately – they always lived on the outskirts of towns, near airports or main roads to cities. In Damascus they had built communities in elevated areas like Mezze; in Homs they lived near government facilities. Places of strategic importance that controlled essential routes.

Majed and I remained close, and we often walked home from school together after the spring holiday. One day when Majed and I were walking home I realized that it was time for evening prayers and decided to stop at the local mosque. Majed joined me in the prayers. Since he seemed very unsure of what to do, I helped guide him through the prostrations.

Syria is composed of a variety of different religious groups. Sunni Muslims are the overwhelming majority, making up 75 per cent of the population; Alawites comprise 8 per cent, Shiites 2 per cent, and Christians 5 per cent.

Shiites believe the Prophet Muhammad should have been succeeded as leader of the Muslim world by his son-in-law Imam Ali and the Prophet's descendants. Shiites continue to commemorate what they consider to be Imam Ali and his descendants' persecution and revere his family, making annual pilgrimages to shrines to the Imam and his eleven descendants. Sunnis don't accept this hereditary succession and greatly outnumber Shiites, constituting nearly 90 per cent of the global community of Muslims. The governments of some Gulf countries – including Saudi Arabia, Bahrain and the United Arab

Emirates – are Sunni, while Iran and Iraq are ruled by Shiites. Shiites and Sunnis pray differently: Sunnis cross their arms, while Shiites keep their arms by their sides. Sunnis observe five daily prayer sessions; Shiites condense the five prayers into three sessions. Shiites are governed by more hierarchical structures, following living religious leaders, whereas Sunnis typically follow scholarly texts penned by past religious leaders.

Alawites are a Muslim minority group accounting for a small percentage of Syria's population, with a few small pockets in Lebanon and Turkey. They practise a unique and little-known form of Islam that dates back to the ninth and tenth centuries. Its secretive nature is an outcome of centuries of isolation from mainstream society and periodic persecution by the Sunni majority. Alawites take a step further in the veneration of Imam Ali, investing him with divine attributes. Other characteristics include a belief in divine incarnation and the permissibility of alcohol. Syria's regime is Alawite, a Shiite offshoot.

Majed's father was waiting for us outside when we finished. 'Majed! I can't believe you. How dare you. Go home now. We'll talk at home, you donkey!' I was shocked. I had never heard Majed's father call him a donkey before – it's a serious insult.

Majed was absent from school for the next two days. He never told me why, and I was afraid to ask. Back then I didn't know that Alawites do not pray like Sunnis and was unaware that prayers were forbidden in the Syrian military. An Alawite officer with a son who prays in a mosque can get into a lot of trouble. I did not know a lot of things at that young age.

*

Towards the end of the school year I told my father that I was bored with school, and he tried to have me skip the third grade. The school administrators were adamantly against this; they said that it was strictly forbidden for me to miss a grade, but that I could skip *three* grades if I passed the sixth grade entrance exam. 'And if he can pass *that*,' they scoffed, 'he'll finish elementary school this year!'

I scored 95 per cent on the entrance exam, but they rejected the result. I scored 93 per cent on the retest, so the school forwarded my scores to the Ministry of Education, which refused our request. My father took my results to the ministry's office in downtown Damascus himself and demanded an explanation. The ministry refused to give one and stood by their decision. In the end, I did not reach the sixth grade until three years later, with the rest of my class. Only then did I find out the real reason for my earlier rejection.

In the first semester of the sixth grade I scored full marks in maths, Arabic and liberal arts, and tied with one other student for the top overall score in the class. Majed was right behind us. In the second semester I outperformed both Majed and the other student, so I was confident that I would top my year. But my final report card left me stunned: I had been docked three points, and in a class that was not even graded, for a final score that left me just below Majed.

Majed apologized to me when he heard the news. He said he knew I had got the top score, but someone had changed the results. He asked me not to hate him. I accepted his apology as I knew that he did not have the power to change anything, but I never forgave the ministry. It was a wound I carried with me for a long time; perhaps even now I cannot forgive them. I came to realize that they had placed Majed above me purely based on his *wasitaa* – connections. Because his father was in the Baath Party and mine was not, because his father was a military pilot and mine was not, Majed would always get a higher score than me. I also realized that the Ministry of Education had stopped me jumping to the sixth grade for the same reason. Was this how education worked in Syria? If so, then there was no point in trying. After this I began to lose interest in my studies.

When I was in the eighth grade, my dear baba passed away from a sudden stroke. I remember the last time I saw my father. It was morning, and I was going to school. He and my mother were having coffee in the kitchen. They were smiling. It was a normal day. When I returned from school that afternoon, I found my sister and three of my brothers sitting, crying. When I asked where Mama was, they said that Baba had a 'health problem' and he was in hospital. My mother and uncle were with him. They told me not to worry. We sat waiting until 10 p.m. in the growing darkness; there was a power cut, a routine occurrence at the time. Then I heard cars arriving outside and got up to look out the window, to see my mother getting out of a taxi in tears. I didn't want to think about what that meant. I prayed it was just a nightmare, that it wasn't real, wasn't what I knew it to be.

I felt then – and still feel today – that sorrow and desperation had overwhelmed him. He was always working so hard for us, trying to keep his family out of poverty. I knew that he was always very tired, even though he hid it well with his smile, his optimism and his boundless positive energy. He always knew exactly what to say to make us laugh and feel that things would be OK. I was

proud that, despite knowing it would have made everything easier for him, he never compromised his principles
by joining the Baath Party.

For my mother his death was devastating. After the
funeral our neighbours were so kind: they took over the
cooking and cleaning, helping her with us kids. Relatives
visited who I met for the first time, and we had plenty of
support. But soon she had to think about what we could
do to survive. My father had written and sold a TV series
when he was alive and completed another one, and my
mother managed to sell it, to tide us over financially in
the immediate future. My father's friends also helped,
and soon all of us were working, over summers and after
school. We all contributed, and we got by – just.

But I became very lost and confused, and very angry.
I found school unbearable and drifted away from my
friends. My father never hit me, and because of this I
never let my teachers hit me either. This was rare in Syria,
where corporal punishment is common. It was especially unusual in my eighth-grade class. We had a teacher
that year who was notorious for using any excuse to hit
students with a wooden ruler. One day not long after my
father died, this teacher stormed into class in a fury and
demanded that all the students hold their hands out to
receive his stinging blows.

I was not a troublemaker at the time and always did my
best to behave, but I had done nothing wrong. So when
the teacher reached my desk, I refused to put out my hand.
'First tell me why you want to hit me. What did I do?'

The teacher was having none of it and tried to grab my
right hand. I used my left hand to push him back. He
swung hard at me with his ruler. I dodged the blow, then
shoved him away even harder with both hands. He gave

up and moved on to the next student. This was the first time I had used violence against a teacher. It would not be the last. Something had changed inside me. Suddenly I felt that the only way to defend myself against violence was with my own fists.

News of my defiance spread like wildfire among the staff. My teacher's failure to hit me became a source of shame for him, and all the other teachers, even the female ones, tried to prove their mettle by landing a blow on me. Since I was no longer concerned with my studies – I knew the results were rigged but I could pass the high school final exams with ease – the rest of my time in school was marked mainly by regular fights and run-ins with my so-called educators.

I began to care more about other things. When my ninth-grade exams ended, I began spending my mornings loitering on the balcony to watch for the daughters of the army officers across the railway line, who would leave around breakfast time on their morning errands. Many of them were beautiful, and since most were Alawite, they did not wear headscarves and dressed more freely than conservative Syrian girls.

One day as I peered towards the Officers' Residence, wondering which attractive girls I would see, I did not spot what I expected. Instead of beautiful well-groomed girls going about their morning errands, I saw officers and their families, some of them still in their pyjamas, rushing from their doors with travel bags and speeding off in their cars or military vehicles. Hundreds of heavily armed soldiers abseiled out of helicopters to take their place until it seemed as if every rooftop, alleyway and street corner in the Officers' Residence was teeming with soldiers.

I rushed inside to tell my mother and my siblings what was happening, but they had heard and seen everything. A Lebanese show was on the TV. Suddenly, the broadcast went dead, and one of my brothers leaped from his chair.

'Sit back down,' my mother said. 'No one goes near the windows, no one goes on the balcony, and no one steps outside the front door. Everyone stays right here until I say you can leave. Understood?' She turned to my sister. 'Ghazwa, why don't you help me make some tea and popcorn? I'm sure we can find something interesting to watch on TV.'

For four whole hours we nervously drank tea and munched popcorn as we waited for news. Nothing appeared on the TV except verses from the Quran, which only made us more nervous. We giggled at each other to try and mask our fear. Finally, at around 3 p.m., Hafez al-Assad's religious spokesman Marwan Sheikho appeared on TV to deliver an important announcement: the Great Protector of the Arab Nation, the Immortal President of our Glorious Syria, the Dear Leader Hafez al-Assad, was dead. Sheikho then burst into tears and began reciting poems describing Father Hafez's uncountable exploits. He was literally shaking from fear and sadness as he read. My family was also shocked and scared. Mama offered a prayer to Allah, asking for his mercy and the protection of Syria, and kept telling us not to leave the house or to go near the windows.

Hafez was born in 1930 in Qardaha, in north-west Syria. In 1946 he joined the Syrian wing of the Baath Party, and in 1971 he made himself president of Syria. The schools, the TV channels and the newspapers had all drummed into our minds the idea that Hafez al-Assad was a god. I recalled the chants at my school, the pictures of Hafez plastered on the walls and all the lectures praising his exploits that we had been forced to listen to. And now he was dead. Our Immortal Leader had passed away just like any other human being.

A few hours later the elaborate choreography to anoint Hafez al-Assad's son began. First the state TV channel announced that Vice President Abd al-Haleem Khaddam would become temporary president of Syria. Then a second bulletin revealed that Khaddam had promoted Hafez al-Assad's second-oldest son Bashar from captain to leadership of the entire Syrian army. More announcements followed in rapid succession. Syria's rubber-stamp parliament met urgently to discuss the minimum age of a president; the Baath Party 'elected' Bashar al-Assad as its leader in a unanimous vote; parliament lowered the minimum presidential age to thirty-four, which was Bashar's exact age; and so on.

As the president and parliament went through the motions of 'electing' a successor, a second charade took place at Damascus University, which two of my older brothers were now attending and had commuted to earlier that day. No classes took place that day. Instead, Syrian intelligence agents herded the students and teachers into a central location and forced them to remain there for a number of hours. When the students and teachers were finally released, Baath Party members were stationed at the university gates with pro-Bashar banners and 'suggestions' that everyone should rally in nearby Umayyad Square.

It was clear that these were anything but suggestions. Students, my brothers included, teachers and government employees were required to attend, while soldiers were ordered to change into civilian clothes and come too. They were told exactly what to shout and where to march. The signs they would hold, with a picture of Bashar al-Assad and a heart symbol, were pre-made and forced into their hands. After a few days of fake rallies, a new phase of intimidation began when the government announced a referendum on whether or not Bashar should be president, the state-controlled newspapers, radio stations and TV channels declaring that it was absolutely imperative for every patriotic citizen to vote. No one wanted to be seen as unpatriotic. We all knew from the Hama massacre of 1982 what could happen to you if you were deemed an unpatriotic citizen.

To no one's surprise, every polling station on referendum day was filled to capacity. Secret service agents urged voters to support Bashar al-Assad's presidency for the sake of Syria then checked their ballot papers and congratulated them on having made the right choice. Assad received overwhelming support in the referendum – 99.9 per cent support, if the official result is to be believed. He took power on 10 July 2000, exactly one month after his father's death, professing himself honoured to have been chosen by the Syrian people.

Like most Syrians, I watched Assad's inauguration speech on TV, at home surrounded by my family. I remember inwardly shaking my head the entire time. Whenever Bashar said 'Hafez' the entire parliament broke into applause. Whenever Bashar used a nice word to describe his father, the entire parliament broke into applause. Whenever Bashar heaped praise on himself, the entire parliament broke into applause. I started secretly calling the Syrian parliament the House of Clappers after this speech because that seemed to be all they were good for.

Despite the farce that brought Bashar al-Assad to power I and many others of my generation saw cause for optimism. His sophisticated manner, his scientific background as an eye doctor and his time spent in the West all made a positive impression. We imagined that Syria would be better off with a youthful president who shared the sensibilities of Syria's younger generation. We thought, or hoped, that Assad's exposure to Western life would mean he would be less iron-fisted than his father, and his first year as president was marked by constant news reports of Syria opening up to the world. There was talk of new trade companies, private banks, private universities and rising young stars in the fields of trade and industry. Satellite TV antennae were legalized for the first time. Two new cellphone companies were founded.

Our elders were far more sceptical, and they found ways to tell us so even though they would not dare say it explicitly. Every time my brothers and I spoke excitedly about Bashar the reformer at the dinner table, my mother fell conspicuously silent. At neighbourhood gatherings, when my friends and I praised Assad as someone who would make Damascus more like London, the adults around us gave us the same sad smile, shook their heads and said, 'We'll see.' They were right to be cynical.

The reforms were largely a sham. Most of the new 'private' companies were owned by Bashar al-Assad's cousin Rami Makhlouf, who monopolized banking, telecommunications, medical equipment, restaurants and any other industry he could think of. Another prominent 'businessman', Muhammad Hamsho, was really just a financial frontman for Bashar's brother Maher. Members of Assad's extended family even controlled the lucrative black markets: drugs, alcohol and prostitutes became openly available at corner stores, and companies specializing in government bribery were established. But who would dare close down a business operated by the Assad family? And all the while, as Assad and his cronies enriched themselves, lower-class Syrians suffered from stagnant wages and skyrocketing prices for basic necessities.

But these issues mattered little to me or to my friends. All we cared about was that there were new and interesting products in the markets. My friends and I salivated at the chance to buy American brands like Pepsi and Coca-Cola, even though the drinks were Syrian-made and tasted suspiciously like the old ones. Upper-middle-class Syrians practically beat down the doors of the new foreign car dealerships, paying an astronomical sales tax of 300 per cent for the privilege of buying a junky Chinese or Iranian car instead of an even junkier Syrian car. The Internet and computers became widely available for the first time. Internet cafés quickly became the trendy location for young Syrians like me to eat, drink and log into chat rooms after school. I became addicted to war-based network video games like *Red Alert* and *Counterstrike*.

These were hopeful years for me, years when I imagined I had a real future in Syria. Only a few more years of high school, I reasoned, and then I would graduate, ace my final exams and embark on a promising career, maybe become an airline pilot. But I was bored listening to the teachers and sick of dodging their punches in the halls, so I would skip classes to play video games and hang out with friends, other boys who had dropped out, older kids and friends from my neighbourhood. We'd play cards, get drunk or try to pick up a girl.

Between my tenth and eleventh grades, a new family moved into the building next door, and I and my friends, who had by now earned a reputation as tough youths, decided that we would try to make a good impression on the new neighbours by helping them to move in their furniture. As my friend and I were carrying a large couch into the apartment, I saw the girl of my dreams. She was wearing a pink T-shirt, blue jeans and a silver necklace, and had long black hair that whipped behind her when she turned her head. Her face seemed to light up when she laughed. I stopped to look at her, forgetting for a moment that I was carrying a heavy sofa.

I found out later that she was named Reem, and that her cousins had just moved into the apartment. From that moment on, I made a point of passing her cousins' building in the hope of meeting her again. But the next time I saw her, she just gave me a nasty look and kept walking. When I saw her a third time, to attract her attention I spat on the ground – a major insult in Syrian culture – and her face turned bright red as she stormed off. It turned out Reem and I went to the same school, so I began to attend more often and looked for her between classes, but she seemed to despise me more each time she saw me. Sometimes she would even return my insult by spitting on the ground in front of me as I walked by.

One day I was talking with my friends between classes when I noticed a boy running sideways in a very strange manner. For a moment I wondered what he was doing, but then he ran straight into Reem with his arms outstretched, so that his hands 'accidentally' fell directly on to her breasts. She screamed. He laughed then flailed his arms some more so that his hands rubbed against Reem's chest and torso, and then he swaggered away to his friends as if nothing had happened. Reem stood frozen in shock.

I was incensed. I would never have accepted this even if it had happened to just any girl, and this was a girl that I liked. I marched up to the boy and tapped him repeatedly on the shoulder until he turned to face me. When he did, I punched him hard, sending him crumpling to the floor. His friends came to his aid, and soon there was a huge melee. It took several minutes before the principal and several teachers were able to break up the fight. When order had been restored, the principal glared at me. 'You again, Kassem? I knew you'd be involved in it! You always are! Tell me, what set you off this time?' I didn't reply.

During the next class break I was talking with some friends when I felt a couple of taps on my back: after months of ignoring me, Reem was finally seeking my attention. She was shorter than I was, so as a joke I swung around with my head raised and pretended not to see her then turned back to my friends. She poked me in the back again, and I looked in her eyes. She smiled.

We were soon chatting regularly, and only three days later we agreed to walk together to and from school every day. Then we started spending all our time together between classes. I would take her to her door before the start of each class, and leave my own lesson early – assuming that I had attended class at all – so that I could meet her at her door when her lesson ended. After two weeks she gave me her phone number, and we worked out a code to call each other's home phones without our parents' knowledge. I knew that her parents wouldn't approve of me. In Syria matches were all about financial security. If a son wanted to get married, he told his parents, and his mother and sisters would look for girls, make appointments with them and check their suitability. Equally, the parents of young girls, and often the girls themselves, cared deeply about the wealth of suitors – it was all about how much money they had, the size of their house. I had nothing, but Reem loved me anyway.

*

When I was in the eleventh grade an official Baath Party delegation made a visit to the school. The staff pulled out all the stops to impress them, including a school assembly that started with the national anthem. As the anthem began to play over the loudspeakers, we all sang the lyrics we had memorized: 'Oh guardians of the homeland, we salute you in peace . . .' But a handful of students from well-connected families were singing very different words at the top of their lungs: 'Oh Layla, my cries yielded no fruits . . .' These were lyrics from the popular Iraqi love song 'Layla and I', and it didn't take long for the students, the staff and the Baath Party delegation to notice them. The students giggled and smirked, the teachers grew noticeably nervous, and the Baath Party delegates' faces turned bright red. I knew that the disobedient students had a stiff penalty in store.

Later that day, a military studies teacher approached me in the hall and said that the principal wanted to see me. Since my grades were slipping, I figured that the principal just wanted to give me another of his pep talks about how I needed to take school more seriously and improve my attendance. I noticed that the guilty singers were sniggering in the hall, but I thought nothing of it.

I walked into the principal's office to find him waiting for me alongside a second military studies teacher and two guidance counsellors. All of them wore very solemn expressions. The principal spoke first, accusing me of mocking the national anthem. I interrupted him, and he slapped me across the face. What followed next was a blur of violence and fury. My fists flew, I threw things, broke things. I cursed the principal, the teachers and counsellors, cursed their families, cursed the school, cursed everything under the sun and stormed out into the hall.

The arrival of the police ended my rampage; in Syria you didn't want to fight the police. However, even though I had just trashed the principal's office and was cursing them every step of the way, the police were surprisingly respectful as they arrested me. I think they must have assumed I was the entitled son of some important Baath Party figure. My adversaries from the principal's office were already at the police station when I arrived. When they saw me, they immediately launched into their accusations: 'This man is a brute and a traitor. He mocked the Syrian national anthem and cursed our glorious leader Bashar al-Assad.'

My mother and older brother Yazid were also there, with Abu Qusai, a lawyer and family friend who had been looking out for us since the death of my father. Abu Qusai had been a good friend of my father's and an admirer of his poetry. He was also an Alawite, and came from a village of military officials. He had excellent connections, and he did a lot to protect my family over the years. Abu Qusai had prepared a sharp retort for the teachers: 'Talk about treachery. It is our patriotic duty to protect the Palestinian people, and yet you tried to beat this poor Palestinian refugee boy? How unpatriotic. Rest assured that I will be filing a complaint with the intelligence services.'

The arguments went back and forth, and the small crowd in the police station quickly grew in size as each side summoned its connections to sway the authorities. In the end, the battle of influence ended in a draw. I returned to school after only a two-day suspension as the cool kid who had left in handcuffs and come back a hero.

Following this incident, my apathy for school hit an all-time high. I failed four courses that year simply because I could not be bothered to take the final exams. Towards the end of the school year, the principal contacted me

through a friend and offered to ensure that I pass the
tenth grade provided I finished my high-school education
elsewhere. I agreed to his offer, and he marked me up,
but at the start of the next school year, I showed up as
normal. The principal was enraged, but I refused to leave
and attended school for the rest of the semester. However,
at the start of the second semester the principal greeted
me in the hall with a huge smile on his face.

'You're not a student here any more,' he told me. 'Your
papers have already been sent to Sahnaya Military School.
Enjoy.'

I was astonished. 'What? You can't do that.'

He sneered. 'You've already been accepted. You know,
you should have been out of here six months ago. I applied
to school after school, but no one would take you. Looks
like you're not a star student any more. Have fun being a
tough guy in Sahnaya.'

I almost wanted to slap him again. Instead, I just
laughed in his face and walked out the door.

Sahnaya Military School felt like a military base. It was
surrounded by a tall concrete wall and had only one
entrance, which was guarded by two soldiers armed with
AK-47s. Many pupils in the school also carried weapons. As the sons of military officers with very high-level
connections, they felt that they could do almost anything
they wanted. Some students from the heavily Alawite
west coast of Syria even bragged about chasing policemen
and shooting at them for sport from SUVs.

One student, who I originally knew only as 'Teacher'
Yasir, left an especially strong impression on me. On my
second day at Sahnaya the school was abuzz with the
news that Teacher Yasir had got into a fight with the local

police. I thought then that Yasir was really a teacher and
would face a serious jail sentence, but then I learned
his full name: Yasir al-Assad. Teacher Yasir was in fact a
student, but because he was a relative of Bashar al-Assad
himself, he was more powerful than any teacher at the
school. Yasir would regularly arrive drunk at nightclubs
and terrorize everyone there. When he picked a fight,
his opponent could not win, and the police were afraid
to break it up. When he approached a girl, she would
not dare to ignore him, and any boyfriend was obliged
to step aside.

Clearly, Sahnaya Military School was a place where
connections were everything – and this was not a place
where I could thrive. Only a few days into the semester I
and ten other students all came late to class. We'd orches-
trated our lateness, so that we could avoid punishment
– how could they punish such a large group for being late?
But, to my surprise, the principal promptly dismissed all
the other students and began shouting at me: 'You donkey!
You moron!' But I had already learned my main lesson
from the Syrian education system: the system was rigged.
I slapped the teacher in the face – the only time I have
ever hit a woman – and dashed towards the rear wall of
the school, leaped on to a water tank, climbed over the
wall, jumped to the ground below and kept running until I
reached the road. I would get a job and earn enough to pay
for private education. I didn't want to waste any more time.

Not long after this I told Reem that I loved her.

She returned my love, and we agreed that I would try
to raise enough money to pay her dowry and then ask
her parents for her hand. By this time I was working the
night shift at a local bakery earning the equivalent of three

dollars a day. Reem's parents had hated me since before I'd dropped out of school. Her mother viewed me as a thug and had warned Reem time and again not to even talk to me, while her father had suggested repeatedly and loudly that I might be attacked if he found out that Reem and I were in a relationship.

There was also a time at school when Reem had not appeared at our agreed meeting point, so I headed towards her house to find out where she was and from a distance saw her speaking with a male neighbour. This caused me to fly into a rage for some reason, and I stamped off. When Reem approached me during the first school break of the day, I walked straight past her as if I hadn't seen her. Reem came up to me again during the second break, this time with tears in her eyes, and I stopped for just long enough to tell her that she was a liar before storming away as she broke down in tears. During the third class break I did not see her but later learned from Reem's friends that she had left school and had attended hospital with a fever. That night one of Reem's friends visited her house and told the entire family that I was stalking her and had caused her illness. Reem was present when her father heard this story, but she was either too frightened or too sick to contradict it. It confirmed to them that I was bad news.

About a year after she had first professed her love to me, Reem called me with her voice shaking. Her parents had been arranging for suitors to appear at their house. She had turned them all down, but a wealthy doctor was coming in just a few days to propose to her, and her family was pressuring her hard to accept the match. She told me that she was not sure she would be able to resist. I hung up the phone, ran to her house and knocked on the front door.

Her father cracked the door open and eyed me suspiciously. 'What do you want?' he snapped. 'Why are you here?'

I was undeterred. 'Look, I know how much you hate me, but I really need to talk to you.'

He paused for a moment, then opened the door all the way. 'Come inside.'

As he escorted me across the threshold, Reem saw me from across the hall, and I gave a wave, but she slapped her cheeks in dismay and hurried towards the kitchen. Her father yanked my arm, pulling me away from her and towards the living-room couch. I sat down, and Reem's mother joined us a few minutes later. 'What are you doing here?' she asked incredulously.

'I'm sorry,' I answered. 'I know you hate me, but I need to talk to you.'

After she sat down, I gave my pitch: 'Look, I know I'm young and I can't offer much. I know that I'm the last person on earth you would ever want to propose to your daughter. I just want to tell you that I really love her and will do whatever I need to do to marry her. I will get a good job, I will treat her well, and I will make her happy.'

Reem's mother seemed convinced; by the time I was finished, she was smiling and nodding in approval. But Reem's father was a different story. He answered cautiously and slowly: 'Thank you for coming here, Kassem. I respect your honesty, and I respect that you came to speak to me as a man . . .' He paused, letting his words hang in the air. I glanced towards the kitchen door, which was frosted glass, and saw that Reem had her ear pressed up against it. Her father got to the point: 'But I must tell you as a man – you will never, ever have anything to do with our daughter. That is my decision, and that is final.' The figure of Reem started shaking behind the kitchen door.

I turned to Reem's mother. 'And what about you?'

Reluctantly she replied, 'The man of the house has spoken. I can't disagree with him.'

The kitchen door opened. Carrying coffee, Reem walked into the room with tears streaming down her face.

'Don't cry, Reem. I don't care what your father says. I know there's a way for us to be together. We'll find a way, even if I have to kidnap you.'

'Kassem!' her father loudly interjected. 'Your coffee has been served. Please, just drink it, and thank you for coming.' I stood up to take a cup from Reem, sat back down next to her mother and drank my coffee with tiny sips so that it would take as long as possible for me to finish. When my cup was finally empty, I thanked both of Reem's parents and left.

There was no way I could marry Reem without paying her dowry, and there was no way I could earn enough for her dowry in Syria. I also began to realize that staying offered few opportunities for a decent future. I was not the only one who felt this hopelessness setting in – other young men, friends and family members felt it too. Throughout my immediate circle, it seemed everyone was searching for a better way to live, and that there was only one way to achieve this. Like my father before me, I needed to seek a solid, well-paying job by looking outside the country where I had grown up. I needed to leave.

My eldest brother, Yazid, already knew this. Yazid had always steered his own course. Although martial arts were technically illegal in Syria – the regime restricted the learning and teaching of sports such as karate and Thai boxing to the military – Yazid harboured a passion for them.

When he was young, he would request 'how-to' martial arts videos from relatives returning from overseas, who would smuggle them into the country. He taught himself the basics then found a coach who was willing to teach him in secret, at a home gym. By the age of twenty-five, he was competing in international tournaments and running his own karate training sessions for friends. Although the police periodically raided his lessons, he had never incurred any serious penalties. Feeling safe, Yazid had set up a Syrian karate federation.

Not long after I visited Reem's parents, I came home to find my mother peering down at the streets from the balcony, her shoulders hunched nervously.

'What's wrong?' I asked her.

'It's your brother, Yazid,' she answered, her voice shaking. 'He left last night without saying anything. He's still not back yet.'

'Maybe he slept over with one of his friends?'

'He usually calls when he does that. I haven't heard from him.'

One day passed with no news, and then a second day. We called all his friends, but no one had seen him. After a third day passed, we moved on to telephoning the hospitals and police stations, but we had no luck. By this point we were panicking. My mother called every single acquaintance she could think of – her old friends from university, the co-workers of my late father – until Abu Qusai again came to the rescue two weeks later. Yazid had been detained by Air Force Intelligence – the most feared branch of the Syrian secret police. Aside from a death notice, this was the worst news we could have possibly received.

We couldn't do anything but wait.

I didn't see Yazid until he was transferred to Adra Prison and allowed family visits three months later. One month after that Yazid was finally released. He returned to us in a state of rage. He kept shouting that he had won a karate trophy for Syria, but it didn't matter what he had achieved or what he would go on to achieve; he'd still be treated like an animal. He was certain that his passion for martial arts was behind his detainment. But this was what he wanted to do, it was his life's work. We tried to calm him as he shouted on, terrified that some-one might hear as he cursed the regime, the military, Air Force Intelligence. But he was done with Syria. He'd had enough. He had no ties other than us, no wife, no children. He wouldn't spend his life cowed, living in fear.

The next morning Yazid packed his bags and left for Lebanon. He later flew to the United Kingdom, where he still lives today, and where he runs a martial arts equip-ment company. I have not seen him in person since that night in the summer of 2006.

My other brothers fared little better than Yazid in setting themselves up inside Syria. Most of them did military service, which was mandatory for males who had reached eighteen years of age. Like everything else to do with the state, the military was corrupt. If you were an Alawite, the armed forces could be a safe career option. You could progress from military service into full-time employment, with a salary, promotion opportunities, a car, a house, power. For non-Alawites, military service meant little more than two years of routine harassment, humiliation and, in one way or another, bribery. There was very little to be learned other than discipline. My brothers were never taught combat or how to handle

weapons. They did, however, learn how to take a beating, how to accept curses on their family, how to dive
into holes for no reason and how to repeat 'Assad for
ever!' and 'Syria is Assad's!' until they were blue in the
face.

There were some exemptions to military service: if
you were an only male child, if you had worked outside
Syria for more than ten years or if you had a disease or
serious illness. The latter was where bribery came in. If
you could afford it, $3,000–4,000 would secure papers
declaring you too ill to serve. Anyone who could pay
this up front did, because it not only saved you from
two years of pointless abuse, but, what with the officers constantly expecting bribes from recruits for leave,
food or other basic rights, you could end up paying
around the same amount of money, if not more, and
still serving.

Because my older brothers could not find the money,
they served their time, but both Razwan and Yeman, like
me, were not the type to accept indignities or insults, so
each got at least a year of extra penalty service for talking
back to officers, disobeying orders, refusing to perform
the degrading tasks that were assigned to them and
getting into fights. As I listened to them describe their
experiences, I knew that I had to avoid military service at
all costs.

At this point I was attending a private school, which
I was paying for myself through the work I was doing at
the bakery. I was studying hard and had resolved to find
work abroad as soon as I had finished high school. A few
weeks after I took my final exams, I walked from home
to a nearby restaurant to eat falafel. The restaurant owner,
a friendly man named Hamadeh from the neighbouring

town of Daraya, greeted me as I entered. We were talking casually when Hamdeh suddenly dropped his tongs, staring past me in terror.

I felt the smack of something hard against the back of my head.

Lost innocence

2006–2008

Three men in plain clothes placed me in handcuffs and dragged me from the shop. When we were outside, they began hitting and cursing me. I was confused and shouted at them that I had done nothing wrong, and then someone kicked me so hard in the groin that I passed out. When I woke up, I was surrounded by at least thirty burly armed men, all of whom were trying to slap, kick or punch me. In between the blows, I managed to lift my head up and look around. I recognized a bus stop across the street; I was only blocks away from my house. This was the last thing I saw before a blindfold was tied over my eyes and I was thrown into a minivan.

Two men kept beating me inside the minivan, but the van did not move. I considered this a good sign. Then the van door opened again and I was pushed out on to the ground for another round of beating and kicking. Finally, I was picked up and carried up some stairs – I counted four flights in total – before being dropped on to a hard floor.

A single set of footsteps entered the room. The floor shook as my captors stamped their feet as they came to attention.

'At ease!' Feet shuffled. The single set of footsteps approached me, and I heard a voice next to my ear. 'Looks like we've caught you, terrorist. You didn't really think you could escape us, eh?'

I didn't understand. I thought it must be some kind of sick joke.

The voice asked if I thought I was tough.

I tried to explain that I was just out for a meal, that I hadn't done anything, but they beat me mercilessly with their feet, with cables and the butts of AK-47s.

After a while I realized that there were other men being tortured nearby. Their screams were louder than any I had ever heard. My assailants stopped at one point to listen and laugh at their cries, encouraging whoever was administering the torture and telling me I was next. My head was slammed on to the floor and I passed out again.

When I came to a second time, they were still beating me, but my mind seemed to have tuned out the pain. It was too busy flickering through past memories, trying to work out why I was there, why I'd been taken. *Maybe it's a boy I fought whose father is an intelligence officer. Maybe it's someone from the school who has a grudge, and told the authorities I'd been cursing Assad. Maybe it's to do with Yazid. Maybe they somehow heard him curse Air Force Intelligence, and they're taking it out on me.*

The beating stopped as abruptly as it had begun. I was pulled to my feet. Someone shouted that they'd 'got another one'. I heard a door open. The screams of the other prisoners became louder. I was pushed towards the door, and I stumbled one, two, three steps. I tried desperately to back away, but my captors dragged me forward.

Suddenly I heard the sound of running footsteps. 'Stop!' cried an out-of-breath voice. 'Take your hands off him. This is an order from above!'

They let me go. I was too weak to stand and I fell to the floor. They stood me up and took off my blindfold. Then I heard a whisper in my ear: 'Do not look up or you will never see light again. Do you understand?' I nodded my head. 'We are about to wash your face. Come with us.'

They walked me to a bathroom, put a towel over my head, and washed and dried my face. Then, with the towel still covering my eyes, they walked me back into the other room and sat me down on a chair facing the wall.

I recalled something that my Alawite friends at school had told me about interrogations: first they beat you, then they give you hope, and then they beat you even more fiercely until they break you. I panicked. I started crying. Hands patted my shoulder. 'Shame on you,' someone said. 'Real men don't cry. Pull yourself together.'

Someone handed me a beer and a cigarette. 'Here – take these and calm yourself down.'

'My mouth is cut inside,' I answered. 'I can't drink alcohol. But I'll take a cigarette.'

Though the cigarette was just a lousy Syrian brand, it was the best cigarette I had ever smoked in my life. It tasted to me as though it had been made from the world's finest tobacco. I was in the middle of my smoke when the men came to attention once more, signalling that someone important had arrived.

'At ease!' a voice said. 'Is this him?'

'Yes, sir!'

Multiple sets of footsteps receded. The new arrival slowly approached me. Without saying a word, he brought his

face right up to mine – I could feel his breath against my
cheek – and then he circled me. His footsteps stopped. I
heard a gun being cocked behind me. I began reciting the
Martyrs' Prayer in my head: *There is no God but Allah . . .*
Muhammad is the Messenger of Allah . . . There is no God
but Allah . . . I felt the gun barrel against my neck. I closed
my eyes and waited.

The man leaned down again and placed his other hand
on my shoulder. 'Talk to me, Kassem.' His voice sounded
like ice. 'How are you, son?'

'I am OK, sir.'

'Sorry about the misunderstanding. You do know we
are brothers, right?'

'Of course, sir.'

'And brothers fight sometimes, right?'

'Yes, sir.'

'And everything that happened today could be considered a sacrifice from you for your country and Master
Bashar, don't you agree?'

'Yes, sir. We are all the Master's loyal soldiers.'

'That's the spirit! You're a good and smart young man.'

'Thank you, sir.'

'I'm sorry that you failed your final exams. Better luck
next year.'

'Thank you, sir.'

'Your late father was such a good guy. He could be quite
hard-headed sometimes, but he was still a good guy.'

'Thank you, sir.'

'Now if I let you go, you must understand that if you
speak even a *word* about what happened here, we will
come for you. You, your family, your friends, and even
your father from his grave. Am I making myself clear?'

'Yes, sir. Very much so, sir.'

'Very good. If anyone asks you what happened, you can just tell them that you got into a fight with your friends. You and I both know that you've had a lot of fights in your life, right?' He chuckled.

'Yes, sir.'

'You have good people looking after you who care about your family. You're lucky that they called us.'

'Thank you, sir.' I had no idea what he was talking about.

I was led out of the room and back down the stairs. Everything was dark, and I felt glass crunch beneath my feet. As we approached the door to the outside, I began to see light again. Someone pushed my head down and removed the towel from my head.

I took a few steps with my head still down, expecting to be shot at any moment, then ran. After a few seconds I saw my brothers, friends and neighbours. I stopped, glanced furtively behind me, and turned all the way around to look back at the building entrance. No one was there. I collapsed on to the ground, weeping. The crowd ran towards me and picked me up off the ground. They hugged me, kissed me, consoled me and thanked God for my survival.

One of my brothers flew into a rage, cursing the people who had done this to me. I panicked. I said loudly that I'd had a fight with some friends, that everything was fine now, that we should all go home. There was an unspoken understanding that I was lying. Everyone suspected what had happened but knew it wasn't safe to discuss it.

When I arrived home, Mama opened the front door with tears in her eyes. I later found out that I had been gone for three hours, though it had felt like years. A neighbour had seen everything, including a young man jumping

off a roof near the restaurant before I arrived, and had
rushed down to tell them that they had the wrong person
– but they hadn't listened. He had then gone straight to
my mother, and she had called Abu Qusai, my brothers and some of our other neighbours. My brothers had
gone out to look for me and come across an area near our
home that had been blocked off by what appeared to be
plain-clothes officers. They suspected I was close and had
waited anxiously until they saw me appear.

When my mother stopped hugging me, I grabbed her
hand, took her to her room and closed the doors, windows
and curtains. 'I want to leave now, Mama,' I whispered. 'I
want to leave this country, if it's the last thing I do.'

I changed after that. It was unavoidable. I refused to leave
the house for weeks on end for fear that I'd be taken again.
I lost weight; my hair began to fall out, and I went days
without sleep. I couldn't talk about what had happened.
I heard stories about others who had been taken, others
who hadn't been as lucky as me and weren't seen again. I
never did find out what had happened to the people who
were in the room next to me. To this day I panic inwardly
every time I hear someone come up behind me.

In the months after my detention, leaving Syria became
my priority. Getting out was my best chance of avoiding
conscription, my only chance of escaping the terrifying
shadow of the secret police and my last hope of getting
a solid job and raising enough money to marry Reem,
though she felt further away than ever.

Since my brother Yazid had already emigrated to the
UK, I asked him for help with a visa. He gave me the
phone number of his friend at the British embassy in
Damascus who had helped him to emigrate. That friend

told me that I should register for an English course in London, bring documentation showing that I owned a house, and produce a bank statement proving that I had at least $10,000 in savings. If I could provide these documents, he said, I could receive a visa within forty-eight hours. But I didn't have that kind of money. Instead, my mother and I resorted to the only real option available to us: forgery and bribes.

It took a full year to find a bank manager and estate agent willing to forge the required documents, but then, when they were ready and I called Yazid's friend, I learned that the British embassy in Damascus had closed. Now there would be no UK visa unless I could get to Amman or Beirut. Getting the visa was a long, complex process. My mother had her Jordanian passport, and every couple of months she would return to Jordan, which she needed to do to collect her pension. Practically all her family lived there, and she would stay for a few days. We decided that when she next travelled to Jordan she would apply for a visa for me, so that I could 'visit' her there. After two months of wrangling with the Jordanian authorities, Mama obtained my visa and travelled back to Syria to get my papers stamped by the Syrian Foreign Ministry. Now I had my Jordanian visitor's visa and forged documents, Mama returned to Jordan a second time and awaited my 'visit'. I would travel to Amman on my visitor's visa, present my forged papers to the UK embassy there and secure a British visa on the pretence that I would be studying in London.

My course in London had already begun by the time I was ready to travel to Amman, so I had to register for a new one. I asked Yazid to enrol me, and one week later received a welcome letter from the university in the mail.

The letter was addressed to a student from Afghanistan. I asked Yazid to call the university a second time, and another letter was sent. This time the letter was confiscated by the Syrian authorities, who feared that a simple envelope containing papers constituted a national security threat. When we figured out what had happened, Yazid called the university a third time, and I finally received the correct welcome letter, but by then my visa to Jordan had expired, so Mama needed to start the Jordanian visa process all over again.

Mama returned to Jordan once more. A visitor's visa was issued, and I received it two weeks later. Finally I was in Jordan. I made my way to the British embassy and submitted my application for entry into the UK. It was rejected within forty-eight hours with no explanation. The refusal letter did not even mention any suspicion of forgery. I wouldn't be joining my brother. I returned to Moadamiya a defeated man, and despite the best efforts of my friends and family to console me, I was miserable.

Reem called me, and I sensed the disappointment in her voice. She had given up, and so had I. We would not be together. Later she married someone else – an older man who had the money to provide the life of comfort that I could not. Like so many other young Syrian men, I felt frustrated, trapped.

In a last-ditch attempt at a decent career, I enrolled at Homs University to study English translation and applied for all the jobs I could find. Eventually, I was interviewed for a security guard position at a hotel in Damascus. This position had possibilities because it was at one of Syria's most upmarket hotels. During the interview I was told about the wonderful career that awaited me, including promotion opportunities and the possibility to work at any one of their hotels across the globe. I accepted the position determined to give it my all.

My job was to keep the building safe, and I quickly took the initiative. I roamed the hotel to memorize the location of every security camera, smoke detector, sprinkler, corner and blind spot. Within three months I was writing English-language reports for the hotel administration on behalf of the entire security staff, and I was viewed as one of the best employees in the department. My managers even counted on me to supervise the security shifts and to deal with VIP guests.

After six months I was eligible to apply for a shift leader's position. Since I was already performing this role even without the title and the extra pay, I was shocked when I was passed over for a less competent employee with terrible English skills. I asked my boss for an explanation. He said only that the other employee was more senior than me, so I continued my hard work, figuring that eventually my time would come. But as I racked up more and more hours, I noticed that employees with less seniority were now overtaking me. Instead of asking my manager for yet another bogus explanation, I did my own digging and found out the truth: it was connections again. The security guards who received promotions all had close ties to the Baath Party and the military.

My work at the hotel opened my eyes to a whole other world – a world of politicians, celebrities and opulence. The hotel was Assad's preferred accommodation for special guests and foreign dignitaries. French President Nicolas Sarkozy, former American President Jimmy Carter and American Senator John Kerry (who made sure to play a game of tennis with Assad each trip) all stayed there when they visited Damascus on official business. Turkish Prime Minister Tayyip Erdogan and Qatari Prince Hamad Bin Jassem al-Thani were especially honoured guests; Assad would pick them up from the airport in his own car, escort them to the Royal Suite on the eighteenth floor, order coffee or tea, and spend at least thirty minutes with them before departing. Assad gave Erdogan and Hamad special attention because they pumped massive amounts of money into the country through investments and trade deals, although when they backed the Syrian people against his murderous thugs in 2011, Assad pretended that Turkey and Qatar were arch-enemies of Syria fomenting terrorism in the country.

Rami Makhlouf, Bashar al-Assad's cousin and financial frontman, was a regular visitor, and often used the hotel as a venue to seal agreements with foreign businessmen. I remember one occasion when the 'Syrian government' (meaning Rami Makhlouf) booked the hotel to receive proposals from real estate developers for the construction of an entire city of five-star hotels and luxury villas on the Syrian coast. Developers from around the world had set up their displays and presentations in the hotel lobby, but when Makhlouf arrived, he walked around for all of ten minutes, signed one contract and left, watched by dozens of businessmen.

One night I was patrolling the guest floors when I received a desperate radio call from a colleague asking me to get down to the main entrance immediately. I ran downstairs, expecting to find an axe-wielding madman. Instead, I saw something much worse: Bashar al-Assad's brother Majed. Majed was younger than Bashar by a year, and notorious for his outrageous behaviour and his cocaine addiction. He had clearly indulged that night.

He had pulled into the hotel driveway at 3 a.m., rolled down the window of his car, pointed at a parked black and orange Lamborghini, and screamed, 'I want that car, let me buy it!'

The car belonged to one of our VIP guests, and we could not simply give it away. My petrified colleague had tried to soothe Majed by pretending that he had called the car's owner and promising he would be down in just a few minutes to conclude a sale, but he had called me instead.

I didn't take any risks. As soon as I learned who it was, I called the night manager, who called the hotel manager, who called Bashar al-Assad's secretary. Under five minutes later, a dozen black cars converged on the hotel, and dozens of huge men in tuxedos climbed out of them to shut down the street. A few of the men approached Majed's car, and after only seconds' conversation Majed got into one of the cars and they all left together.

I saw a lot of corruption at the hotel, but prostitution angered me most because I saw the victims in front of me every day. We tried to deter the practice by restricting access to the guest floors to those who had paid for their rooms, thereby forcing guests receiving 'companions' to pay for a whole second room, but money was no problem for many of our guests, and prostitution was popular among the hotel's clientele. The companions of certain army officers became regular visitors. I remember one woman in particular, Nancy. She looked around twenty-two years old. Sometimes Nancy serviced three different clients in one night, each of them two or three times her age. I wanted to help her, but how could I? I had no power and no money to change things for myself, let alone her.

*

In 2008 Syria hosted the Arab League summit, and several heads of state chose to stay in the hotel instead of the special villas that Assad had built for them. The Syrian Republican Guard and the Political Security Directorate were tasked with ensuring their protection. The security services reserved the entire hotel for a week, evicted all the guests and forced most of the hotel employees to take a vacation for the period of the summit. I was among the few allowed to remain after passing a background security check.

Political Security bosses arrived two days before the summit to scout out positions for their snipers. Two generals and several officers, alongside my boss and two senior hotel security supervisors, toured the hotel for three whole hours without finding suitable locations. One of these generals, Ayman Harrouq, was closely connected to the Assad family and known throughout Syria for his extremely hot temper. Harrouq was livid when he returned to the hotel lobby after his failed tour. He was cursing and shouting at how idiotic and incompetent the hotel's security staff were when his eyes suddenly fixed on me, and he demanded that I help him. I told him I knew the perfect spots, to which he shouted I was to take him there immediately.

He and I set off, accompanied by my boss and several officers as I raced to recall all the rooftops I had sneaked on to to smoke cigarettes and enjoy the Damascus view. At one point Harrouq literally kicked my boss and the officers away, leaving just me and the other general. My boss had taken Harrouq to the main rooftops, which were either too high or too low for snipers, but they had completely forgotten about the smaller roofs on the middle levels that were the perfect height. When I showed these to the general, he was overjoyed. He hugged me like a Russian bear, compressed my chest until I could barely breathe, and dragged me by my shoulder to the main lobby. Releasing me in the middle of the lobby he unleashed his fury at my boss.

'This employee of yours should be your boss. *You* do not deserve to be *his* boss. If I ever hear from anyone that you have treated him badly, I will come and kill you – do you hear me?'

My boss hated me from that moment on, but he was afraid to say a word against me.

One evening in late December 2009 I came home to find my mother looking worried. My younger brother Waddah, who was almost thirteen now, had a bad fever. The doctor had diagnosed it as nothing serious and had given him some antibiotics, but he wasn't recovering. Over the following days my brother's health continued to deteriorate until he could barely walk. We took him to hospital, where they told us that Waddah might have a rare blood virus, and needed to have blood tests and stay in hospital until the results of the tests were known. That night, however, my boss insisted I work or I'd be fired. It was New Year's Eve, and they were busy – he would accept no excuses. While my family stayed with Waddah, I went to work. Early in the hours of the morning, as the new year dawned, I received a call from my brother Raylan. He urged me to come home immediately. There I found my family and neighbours in tears. They told me that my dear brother Waddah had passed away.

I now became a very different employee. Disillusioned again, I knew I had no future at the hotel. I began to mess around. My main goal was to have fun and do the bare minimum to receive my pay. If a guest told me to have their car valeted, I would pretend to park it, then speed out of the garage and drive as fast as I could through downtown Damascus. Whenever the $10,000-a-night Royal Suite was unoccupied, I would use it myself and sleep naked in the bed. I even made a point of smoking around the hotel guests, although the hotel was smoke-free. Who was going to stop me?

My course at Homs University was also unstimulating. I felt I already knew everything and doubted it would take me anywhere in this country of no opportunity. My days were a meaningless cycle of study and work, commuting from home to Homs, to Damascus and back home again.

No going back
December 2010–October 2011

The Arab Spring changed everything.

On 17 December 2010 I was playing cards at a friend's house when one of his family members burst into the room. 'Look what's happening in Tunisia!' We rushed to the TV, which was showing the satellite station Al Jazeera, and saw that a poor fruit vendor from a small Tunisian town had set himself on fire after an altercation with a police officer. A young man desperately trying to make a living, he had been beaten and harrassed by the police, and felt humiliated and hopeless. He no longer cared about his own life so had made a final suicidal gesture. We whistled and shook our heads; this was one of the craziest stories of the year. Then we went back to our card game.

A few days later we heard more about the vendor, Muhammad Boazizi. Protests over his death were spreading like wildfire across Tunisia. Clashes with police were now taking place in the streets. Still, we dismissed the protests as just another wild story from the Arab world. I was barely keeping up with the news back then and heard nothing about Tunisia in the days that followed, so I assumed that the protests had simply died down.

When my friends and I learned a few weeks later that the protesters had overthrown the government of Tunisia, we were stunned. We could never have imagined a democratic revolution in an Arab country. We were especially shocked that the Tunisian military had not chosen to support the Tunisian dictator, Zine al-Abedine Ben Ali. But I was doubtful. I believed that Ben Ali would recover, that the reports were false, or that he had only lulled the protesters into a false sense of security before initiating a huge massacre.

However, in the days that followed we not only received confirmation that the stories were true, we also learned that protests had begun in Egypt, the most populous Arab country. We knew then that the Arab Spring was a profound phenomenon and that it would affect the entire Middle East. After Egyptian protesters brought down dictator Hosni Mubarak in just three weeks, our only question was which country would be next. Would it be Saudi Arabia? Morocco? Jordan? Yemen? When I spoke to close friends, those I really trusted, we could only joke that the Arab Spring might reach Syria. We were afraid, as we had been since the day we were born, to discuss the prospect of regime change in Syria. Yet we had newfound hope that change would one day come.

After the fall of Hosni Mubarak, Facebook pages began to appear calling for a mass protest in Syria. This demonstration, set for 14 February 2011, was to honour deceased Lebanese Prime Minister Rafik Hariri, who had been assassinated for defying the Syrian government's military occupation of Lebanon. But the protest was a dud; only a few protesters tried to assemble in downtown

Damascus, and they were promptly detained, beaten and sent home.

Three days after the failed protest, my friend Moatasem called me on his cellphone. I thought he was calling from the Hawiqa Square area in Old Damascus, where he worked in a lingerie shop and where I would sometimes visit him.

'Hey, Moatasem! What's up? How's the underwear going?' I joked.

He shushed me. 'Quiet! Just listen.'

I listened and I heard the unthinkable. A crowd of people – what seemed to be a large crowd – was shouting, 'Syrians will not be humiliated!' It sounded like a protest chant.

The Arab Spring had reached Syria.

I suddenly thought to myself, *How do I know if this is really my friend Moatasem? Maybe this is the secret police looking for an excuse to finish me off.* After thirty seconds of silent deliberation, I hung up.

That evening I rushed to Moatasem's house and asked him what had happened. He showed me the video of the protests he had taken on his cellphone, then deleted it immediately. If he was found in possession of such footage, it would be a death sentence. Later that night I tuned in to Al Jazeera and saw footage of the same protest. I was astounded. Had there really been an Arab Spring protest in Syria? How had the protesters dared?

My friends' discussions of the Arab Spring took on a new urgency and intensity after the Hawiqa Square protest. When some of my friends talked about it, I looked into their eyes and saw eagerness, and I knew that they were only waiting for the right moment to act. Other people I knew argued that Assad was a great leader, not like the dictators who had been overthrown. When I looked into their eyes, I saw fear and fury; they knew that large-scale protests might happen, but they were determined to prevent them. I tried my best to learn what others were thinking without sharing my own views, but deep down I too was hoping for revolution.

On 15 March 2011 I got my wish, though as with everything it came at a price. Syrians in the southern city of Deraa staged massive demonstrations against the detention and torture of some schoolchildren who had written the Arab Spring protest chant THE PEOPLE WANT TO BRING DOWN THE REGIME on a wall. This was a definitive moment, the moment at which the regime showed itself capable of the extraordinary cruelty, violence and disregard for human rights that it had so far kept under wraps. It was exposed, and across the country citizens were ready to rise. Something was taking shape in Syria, you could feel it in the air. I had spent so long thinking this day would never come, and when it did, I was unprepared. I couldn't believe it. But I knew that my incredulity and disbelief were no excuse. If children in Deraa could call openly for the downfall of the regime, I had no excuse to keep silent.

My hometown of Moadamiya joined the protests three days later, on the afternoon of 18 March 2011. Around 300 people marched through the town centre chanting for the resignation of Moadamiya's mayor and calling for the return of municipal lands confiscated by the regime. I heard them when they gathered at the main square about fifty metres from my house, and I ran up to my rooftop to watch the scene.

For about twenty minutes the protesters chanted undisturbed. Then, five large buses arrived, and plain-clothes regime agents who looked and acted just like the ones who had beaten and tortured me flooded out on to the streets. We called these plain-clothes agents the *Shabiha*. They were thugs, ruthless men loyal to the Assad regime. They had been created by Assad's father Hafez in the 1980s to do his dirty work. Mostly Alawites, the closer they were related to the Assad family the more vicious they were. On this occasion they were carrying clubs, crowbars, swords, shotguns and AK-47s. They also deployed SUVs and fire trucks, using their hoses as water cannons. Eventually, the *Shabiha* cornered the protesters in front of the municipal building with the water cannon, shooting bullets into the air.

I thought then that the protest would end, but when the *Shabiha* began insulting the protesters, the enraged crowd fought back. Hundreds of bystanders joined the crowd, more *Shabiha*-filled buses arrived, and ambulances started removing the injured. The ambulances left with only *Shabiha* because no protester wanted to be taken to an official hospital, which were controlled by the regime. After nine hours, at around midnight, the *Shabiha* managed to impose a total curfew, and the streets fell silent.

Not a single member of my family slept that night. My mother, my brothers, my sister and her husband, who lived nearby but had been with us that evening, we all stayed glued to the television for news on the protests. Many satellite stations were covering the events. Al Jazeera interviewed an anonymous eyewitness I recognized as my friend Waseem, as he described the street clashes that had just taken place blocks from my house. Friends called me late into the night for information about the protests, but I was afraid to say anything over the phone, so I lied and said that I knew nothing about them because I had been out of town.

That night, for the first time in many years, I and my entire family dared to hope that freedom was possible in

Syria – not in a decade or a generation, but in a year, maybe even a month. Even though we were frightened and we expected many awful things to happen, that was not enough to erase our joy.

The next day Moadamiya was packed with *Shabiha*, and community leaders went to the Mezze airbase to discuss the protests with Air Force Intelligence chief Jamil Hassan. Hassan expressed regret at the *Shabiha*'s harsh response to the protesters and assured the notables that Moadamiya residents had rights and that those rights would be respected. But he concluded with a threat: 'Make sure that such events never happen again. We will not be so forgiving next time.'

On the ground in Moadamiya the *Shabiha* took the same dual approach. In some cases, when residents were caught outside after curfew, regime agents would sidle up and escort them in an almost-too-friendly manner: 'Hi there, friend. What a fine night! Where are you off to? Don't worry, wherever you're going, we are here to serve and protect you.' But in other cases agents armed with AK-47s would scream at any resident they saw on the street: 'There's a curfew! Get the hell off the streets, you dog! If you don't get back inside your house, I'll go inside and rape your sister!'

Three days later, on 21 March 2011, Moadamiya activists, including some of my friends, staged another protest on the occasion of Syrian Mothers' Day. This time there were 4,000 people marching instead of 300, and they were not just calling for local reforms, but shouting, 'Deraa, we are with you until death!'

Watching these protests from my balcony, I felt like I was on fire. I wanted nothing more than to join them and to scream for my freedom. I felt liberated, as if I had just been sprung from jail. I moved towards the front door.

My mum shouted, 'Where are you going? What are you thinking?'

I stopped in my tracks.

'Kassem, think of your brothers! Think of your sister! Think of your family! If you protest, they will come after us all, and we cannot afford anything bad to happen to any of you!'

It was a time of heightened but mixed emotions. I knew my mother was happy about the revolution, and about the protests – to see people speaking their minds finally, to see people objecting to the conditions that had led my father to an early death – but her elation was shot through with fear. We had always existed on the margins, as Palestinian-Syrians. The previous day, in an effort to turn the popular unrest towards people like us, one of Assad's spokeswomen, Bouthaina Shaaban, had claimed that Palestinian refugees had instigated the protests in Deraa. My mother wanted us to wait until it was safer to join the protests, if such a time ever came. For me it was impossible not to be swept up in the momentum that was gathering, to feel like I could finally do something after years of being oppressed and ignored. But I had to respect my mother and to think of my family. So I stayed.

It took only an hour before the protesters were surrounded by more regime security vehicles than I could count. I stood on my balcony and watched the *Shabiha* fan out into the streets to crack down. Nevertheless, the demonstrations grew steadily after the successful Mothers' Day protest. By early April over 10,000 people were protesting in Moadamiya on a daily basis, with numbers exceeding 15,000 on Fridays. Even though the *Shabiha* attacked every demonstration, the protesters were undeterred.

On 10 April my friends and I decided to take a break from the tense atmosphere in Moadamiya and spend a day in downtown Damascus. We were walking towards the bus stop near my house when I saw some cars surround and stop a taxi. *Shabiha* poured out of the cars and threw open all the taxi doors, yanked out the driver, whom they began beating, and then pulled out the two women from the back. The thugs ripped off the women's headscarves and threatened to rape them. The women tried to get away, but the *Shabiha* caught them and grabbed their breasts. The women were screaming. Passers-by yelled, but the agents ignored the cries and dragged the women into a nearby building lobby as other *Shabiha* closed and blocked the doors. I could no longer see what was happening, but I could still hear the women's screams.

I felt worse at that moment than I had ever felt in my life, even when I was being tortured. I felt so powerless. I wanted to defend the women, but I did nothing for fear that my mother and sister would face the same fate if I intervened. There was nothing I could do. With my blood boiling, I kept staring in the direction of the screams. A friend tugged at my sleeve. I did not move. A passing security agent saw where I was looking and shouted at me to move on. My friend pleaded with me to leave. I turned and walked away without saying a word.

I did not go to Damascus that day; I went to a nearby friend's house and told him that I needed to make an urgent phone call. When I got home I went up to the roof, collapsed and cried like a baby. Even though those women were not my family, I felt as if I had failed them somehow. That was when I decided I could no longer obey my mother's pleas to stay away from the protests. But before I took any serious steps I tried to ensure that my mum and sister were safe. That night I told my mother what I had witnessed and suggested that Ghazwa, my sister, leave Syria for the time being. Ghazwa had two young children by this time, and we all felt the situation would only get worse before it got better, and she was vulnerable. My mother agreed and began making inquiries for Ghazwa to move abroad, contacting her family in Jordan to see if they could help. I tried to persuade my mother to leave at this time as well, but she refused.

On 22 April 2011 I left Moadamiya along with my brothers and some friends to spend the night at a friend's villa in the nearby town of Jdidet Artuz. We were seeking an escape from the tense atmosphere and a place where we could talk freely. We stayed up late into the night discussing events in our town. At around 5 a.m. I missed a call from my friend Waseem, who was fast emerging as a leading activist in Moadamiya. I attempted to return the call, only to find that his cellphone line was dead. I tried his landline, but this was also dead. Finally, I called my home number, but again nothing. Something was very wrong.

For the next four hours my friends and I made call after call to friends, neighbours and family, to no avail. We were preparing to go back to Moadamiya to investigate when my friend's father pulled into the driveway. He was an army officer who had been deployed in Moadamiya and had witnessed the events of the previous twelve hours. He informed us that the town was now considered a closed military zone by the regime. All communications were cut, routes to and from the town were blocked, mosques were surrounded and tanks were in the streets. Thousands of soldiers, including elite forces from the 4th Division and the Syrian Republican Guard, were on patrol inside and around the town. Even army officers were technically forbidden to leave; he had only managed to return home after a long shouting match with his superiors.

But he also told us that the ordinary residents of Moadamiya were fighting back. In the largest demonstration in the history of Moadamiya, over 20,000 people had taken to the streets, with women joining the protests in large numbers for the first time. The regime had killed fifteen people by firing live ammunition, and pandemonium prevailed in the town. If we tried to return, we would be stopped, and if we persisted, we would be arrested, or worse. We stayed in Jdidet Artuz for the entire next day before we finally decided that it was safe to go back.

As my friend's father escorted us through the checkpoints, it did not feel like I was returning to the town that I had grown up in, more like I was crossing the front lines of a war zone in a foreign country. I saw more tanks and soldiers than I had ever seen before in my life. Instead of young children running happily through the streets, the pavements were smeared with blood, the quaint old mud houses of Moadamiya scarred with bullet holes.

My brothers and I went straight home after clearing the checkpoints. My mother cried when she saw us, and thanked God that we had not been in Moadamiya during the occupation of the town. At home with my younger brothers, she had been terrified.

In the days that followed, checkpoints appeared on all of the main streets in Moadamiya, especially the streets leading towards downtown Damascus. Meanwhile Assad's forces occupied a number of other towns and used live ammunition on protesters just as they had in Moadamiya. Though the crackdowns only made it even more risky to protest, hearing news of them convinced me that I could no longer wait to act.

I bought some clothes unlike those I normally wore and a pair of plain sneakers, even though I preferred colourful shoes. I then lied to my family and told them I was going out to play football, but when I left the house I changed into my new clothes, put on my plain shoes, covered my face with a cloth to further disguise my identity, and made my way to the protest square.

The atmosphere was electrifying. We would curse Assad, chant for freedom, invoke Allah and cry, 'The people and the army are one!' or, 'Shame on he who shoots his own people!' Gunshots would crackle through the air at every protest, and we would run for cover, only to reassemble and resume our chants as soon as the gunfire subsided. While the shots scared us, they also increased our will to resist.

Over time we came to recognize the sound of each type of weapon. Long bursts of gunfire were actually safer; they meant the security forces were firing over our heads with machine guns. When we heard individual gunshots, though, we ran for our lives, because these were live bullets fired directly into the crowd. These single shots would often be followed by bullets whizzing past our heads, windows shattering behind us and the wounded cries of Moadamiya's latest protest casualties.

I did not attend the protests on a regular basis. My mum and Ghazwa were still at home, so I did not feel free to take all the risks that I wanted. Sometimes I would miss the protests for weeks on end out of concern for my family. Other times I could not even get to the protest square because the regime had set up a flying checkpoint at the corner of our street. A clever tactic, these checkpoints would appear suddenly, unpredictable in time and location. Three to four patrols would converge on a small area and check IDs, intimidate people and arrest them for minor or made-up offences. If you ran or tried to avoid them, they would shoot. The only option was to walk up to them, let them look at your ID and interrogate you, and pray you wouldn't be arrested.

Because our family home was very near the Officers' Residence, it was rare for the *Shabiha* to raid the block. I used this advantage to turn it into a safe house for anti-Assad activists. My friends Waseem, who helped establish the Moadamiya local council, and Adnan, who would later help initiate the armed resistance in Moadamiya, frequently took shelter in my apartment when regime raids were under way. When Waseem and Adnan knocked on my door, I knew that they were running for their lives, but we greeted each other casually, as if nothing was wrong, to conceal the truth from my family. We played cards, drank tea, watched TV and pretended that this was just another day, in the hope that if the *Shabiha* ever broke down our door, they would find nothing amiss.

As April turned to May and the protests persisted, the regime grew steadily more brutal. We began to hear very loud, solitary shots which always found their targets and whose victims usually died immediately from wounds to the head, neck or chest. These came from snipers, but it was impossible to know if they were aiming at particular people, or the killing was random, just another act of intimidation. Even the funerals of protesters were not safe. Regime snipers would specifically target these gatherings. Sometimes snipers even shot pallbearers, sending the deceased's body tumbling to the ground and adding to the distress of friends and family.

My dear sister Ghazwa left Syria with her husband and young children in June 2011, after my mother's extended family secured her a teaching job in the United Arab Emirates. By this point my mother's determination to stay was also wearing thin, and she was trying to find us all safe passage out. The regime had begun using barrel bombs, which inflicted dozens of casualties on both protesters and ordinary civilians. Though they claimed unidentified so-called terrorists were behind the blasts, it just wasn't possible.

My brothers and I persuaded my mother that Assad's escalating brutality meant it was time for her to leave the country, and that we would follow when we could, so she left for Jordan in August 2011. We told her it would be easier for her to help us leave from outside, and that she could do little from Moadamiya, but I think she knew we had no intention of following her. She suspected that we wanted to at least try to contribute to the movement for change, so that she and the rest of the family living in exile could return. After she left, she would regularly call us from Jordan and warn us to stay out of trouble, and we would have heated arguments with her every few weeks over whether or not she should come back to Syria. Somehow, my brothers and I were able to convince her that while it was best for us to remain behind, she would only make our situation worse by returning.

Moadamiya suffered some 200 martyrs during the first seven or eight months of protests, which is a huge number for a small town. More than 5,000 civilians, including women, children and old people, were also detained by the regime in Moadamiya during this time. Sexual assaults on women like the one I witnessed in April became common. In a foreshadowing of the siege that would later crush our town, the regime began cutting off water, power and access to medical services on a regular basis. Car bombs became more frequent. Because we lived right on the border between the Officers' Residence and Moadamiya's civilian neighbourhoods, I would regularly hear mortars fired from Mezze airbase or the 4th Division's mountain headquarters whoosh over my head towards the centre of town.

As the death toll from regime attacks on funerals increased, Moadamiya residents stopped using the main graveyard. Instead, we created a new cemetery in the woods, which we called the Martyrs' Graveyard to commemorate those who had been killed in opposition to the Assad regime. My friends and I told morbid jokes about this cemetery, quipping that it was one of the reforms Assad had promised in response to the protests. Instead of living above ground, people now lived below ground; instead of building houses as we once did, we now built graveyards.

One day in late 2011 I came home to my apartment building to find a blackened facade and blasted-out windows. Whole sections of the walls were missing, and pieces of shredded furniture and shattered glass lay strewn all over the living-room floor. My brother told me that a car bomb had exploded down the street earlier in the day. Only a few minutes before the bomb went off, he had gone into the kitchen because he wanted a glass of water. Those few minutes were all that separated him from death.

Most of my brothers now began to make plans to leave. Between the car bombs, the bombardments, the cuts in basic services and the regime's random arrest raids targeting young men, they felt that it was simply too dangerous to stay. My brothers were in good company. By the end of 2011, over 70 per cent of Moadamiya's population had left for so-called safe areas – where there were no protests. Many good friends of mine bade me farewell around this time, arguing that they were concerned for their families, that the situation had grown too violent or that they just could not live in such conditions.

Some residents who stayed behind were simply afraid to pass through the checkpoints, lacked the funds to leave or preferred to die in their homes; it's hard for me to explain what it was that kept me there. I think it was something to do with the new purpose the protests had given me, and I know that a lot of other young men felt that way too. We thought we could change things, create a future for ourselves where before there was none. Finally, we were a part of something.

The next step in the revolution was building a defence force. This was the start of the Free Syrian Army. I knew nearly every founding member of the FSA in Moadamiya. Most were my age and old friends from my school or my neighbourhood. As we watched Moadamiya slowly empty, we engaged in confusing and agonizing discussions over whether to take up arms. No one wanted to fight for the sake of fighting; we all knew that taking up arms would place us on a very difficult path. But we were unwilling to face the cost of not fighting. We refused to sit back and watch as the regime raped women, arrested and tortured civilians and emptied our town of its residents. Those who had been arrested or had lost family members were especially eager to fight back.

But changing from a civilian to a fighter means crossing an emotional boundary. I didn't feel confident about making that transition myself, but I did my best to contribute. I used my connections with Alawite former classmates to smuggle in whatever weapons I could.

Procuring weapons turned out to be surprisingly easy, at least in those early days; the regime seemed to want us to get them. We all noticed that, while activists trying to sneak past regime checkpoints were almost always caught, trucks carrying barely concealed guns and ammunition were able to reach Moadamiya safely. Later we would see the ease with which we were able to arm ourselves as a tactic employed by the regime. Of course they wanted us to fight. If we fought, they could label us terrorists and justify their attacks on us. They were looking for an excuse.

I thought I knew a lot about America; I had read the *Reader's Digest*, I had read history books, and I had learned about American culture by watching dozens of English-language American movies. I told my friends that the United States had a million reasons to bring Assad down. After all, Syria was strategically located in the Middle East and would be more open to Western influence after Assad was gone. Assad had trained al-Qaeda in Iraq to kill American troops, so there was bad blood between Assad and America, and Syria also had close ties to Russia, an old US rival. The fall of Assad would therefore be a major strategic gain for the United States. Over and over I reassured my friends that it was only a matter of time before American help was on the way. I truly believed this.

If I and all my friends could travel back to those days and relive them again, I don't think we would have made a different choice. We chose to stand up to Assad, confident that the Americans would at least come to our aid with a no-fly zone like they had in Libya, which resulted in the fall of Muammar Gadaffi. Syrians across the country held huge demonstrations for a no-fly zone in October 2011. If we had known then that the world would be so deaf to our cries, we might have spent more time learning how to fight – how to establish supply lines, how to create bomb shelters, how to store supplies for an extended siege – but we still would have taken up arms.

The Free Syrian Army in Moadamiya began operations in October 2011 with an attack on Air Force Intelligence Lieutenant Abu Jaafar. This was a turning point in the war for me. Abu Jaafar was one of the first regime officers to man checkpoints in Moadamiya. He was notorious for humiliating people and for sexual assaults, which included the rape of women inside their own homes. One day, as his convoy was approaching the main protest mosque, FSA fighters ambushed Abu Jaafar's vehicle, killing him. They then took some of his patrol hostage for a number of hours before sending them back alive with the following message: 'We don't want the situation to escalate. We only attacked Abu Jaafar because he was humiliating us. But from now on, if you continue to humiliate us, we will defend ourselves.'

The atmosphere in Moadamiya following Abu Jaafar's killing was more tense than ever as we braced ourselves for the regime's response.

Last meetings
January–December 2012

I met Majed, my childhood friend, in the winter twilight near the railway tracks that separated Moadamiya town from the Officers' Residence. On one side of the tracks were Syrian citizens being slaughtered for demonstrating in support of democracy; on the other side were their killers, Alawite soldiers and officers working day and night to crush their revolution. Majed was one of these soldiers, but he had also been my friend. Though our paths had taken very different turns, his family had been so supportive in the wake of my father's death, and he and I were like brothers.

Majed had recently graduated from a military academy and was set to become a fighter pilot. I had once dreamed of becoming a fighter pilot; before the revolution I would have envied Majed's job. Over the years he had regaled me with his exploits, such as the time he changed his flight plan mid-journey to land in his girlfriend's village. I loved hearing stories like these, even though I knew they could never happen to me. Majed never told me that he had shot at protesters, but I knew. Even after the revolution began, I would go to his house and, when we were alone, we would speak about events in the country. I would try to convince

Majed that there was a real democratic revolution in Syria, but he would talk just like every other *Shabiha*, telling me it was a conspiracy, that the demonstrators were paid by Qatar or were on drugs, that videos of protests were fabricated.

We had many conversations over the span of a few months, up until the killing of Abu Jaafar.

The regime's response was to triple security patrols and hit Moadamiya with heavier and heavier bombardments. Patrols began to include not only *Shabiha* buses, but also newer and more fearsome vehicles mounting Iranian-made heavy machine guns. They would arrest residents on the street, throw them into rubbish bins and take their IDs, warning the arrestees that their entire families would be taken and all their female relatives raped unless they were still there when they returned, sometimes days later. One friend of mine refused to leave the bin they threw him in. We found him sobbing and tried to pull him out, but he clung to its sides as if for dear life.

More friends packed their bags, collected their families together and said goodbye to Moadamiya for good. The bravest told only their families to leave, but stayed behind themselves to fight back.

On that cold evening in January 2012 fighting was raging in Damascus, Homs, Daraya, Edlib and Hama.

The Free Syrian Army in Moadamiya was gathering steam. I was now established in my role as middleman, reaching out to my Alawite contacts from school, offering bribes in exchange for help smuggling food and medicine into the town. My apartment was also an ideal vantage point from which to monitor regime troop movements, so I was able to warn the FSA of approaching patrols. I never told Majed about my activities, but I suspect he knew, just as I knew he was shooting protesters.

I felt this was my last chance to convince Majed to defect before the violence spun totally out of control. I did not have high expectations – Majed had stood by Assad despite hundreds of civilian deaths, so why would to see such conversation with me change his mind – but I ~~to see such~~ ____ him not to try. I could not bear

We exchanged pleasantries for a ~~wng~~ side of the fight. wife and family and discussed his latest flying exploits, and then I began to talk about what Bashar was doing – killing protestors, torturing people to death. Majed's expression hardened. He told me we were friends, that he didn't want anything bad to happen to me, but that there would be no mercy – the order had been given to strike and to strike hard until all enemies of Syria surrendered or died. He only wavered slightly during our long conversation, but in the end he said he could not turn his back on his people.

'We are all Syrians,' I protested.

'You don't understand, Kassem. Many Alawites hate Assad too, but we still fight for him, because if he falls, they're coming for all of us.'

I tried to argue against this, but when he asked if I knew any Alawites fighting for the rebels, I didn't answer.

He invited me back to his house, to catch up – on anything, he said, but politics – but I shook my head. 'I'm sorry, Majed, but I really must be going. I'll see you later, inshallah.'

That was my last meeting with Majed. Every time I've seen an Assad plane drop its payload since then, I've wondered if Majed was the pilot.

*

The armed resistance in Moadamiya developed slowly, in painful stages. We knew no tactics; no one had ever taught us how to shoot or attack in formation. As a result the first FSA operations were often suicidal snotgun group of fighters would attack a ta~~ AK-47s. A single fighter ~~~~~. These 'operations' often would confro~~~ ~~~only in showing the regime that the fighters of succe~~~ the Free Syrian Army were not afraid to die – but die they did, and their amateurism may have encouraged further regime atrocities by making it seem like Moadamiya was easy prey.

Everything changed after army officers began to defect at the start of 2012. These men knew how to use weapons effectively, how to carry out guerrilla attacks and how to manufacture explosives. They taught us that we should not confront Assad's forces directly; we should let convoys pass, and ambush the soldiers from the sides and rear to inflict maximum casualties. They also cautioned us not to confront the regime when it launched a full ground invasion. Instead, we should set landmines to blow up their vehicles then disappear, take shelter in the countryside, melt into the crowds, or sneak away into neighbouring towns until the government forces had left.

Through an ambush here, an ambush there, the FSA gradually forced the regime to concede whole sections of Moadamiya to the revolution. One morning I was walking to a friend's house when I saw a cloud of black smoke billowing from a location near the field hospital. With my friend I ran to investigate. We arrived at the site and saw a massive green *Shabiha* bus, larger than any we had yet seen, burning in the middle of the street. The FSA had repulsed a *Shabiha* assault, and inflicted heavy casualties before burning the vehicle. The *Shabiha* bus was too large to be moved, so it remained in its spot as a symbol of the town's steadfast refusal to submit.

Normal life was over. With residents leaving in droves and regular power outages, nights descended with a grave-like darkness. The only sounds that punctuated the silence were gunshots or, occasionally, threats echoing from the loudspeakers on the mosques. At times my friends and I would try to escape the oppressive atmosphere, and in February 2012 we headed to a friend's family villa nearby in Jdidet Artuz just when the Assad regime decided to strike.

Not long after we arrived, I began receiving phone calls from inside Moadamiya warning us that the regime had surrounded the town with large numbers of troops and tanks. The callers also said that checkpoint security was very tight and that all residents had been barred from entering or leaving. I called my brothers. Earlier, fearing the worst, my second-eldest brother Razwan had evacuated my remaining family to a friend's house in Mezze in Damascus, using his contacts at the state TV agency where he worked to pass through checkpoints unmolested. When I got through to Razwan, he urged me to stay out of Moadamiya for as long as the town was surrounded.

Over the course of the day the news from Moadamiya grew steadily worse. First I received calls indicating that the town was being bombed heavily, then friends called from the outskirts of Moadamiya, on lines with very poor reception, to report that a massacre was under way and that they had fled from the town centre to escape the slaughter.

When we returned to Moadamiya two days later, using the cover of twilight to sneak back into the town from

Highway 40, the smell of burned flesh pervaded the town. Charred corpses were everywhere: in the supermarkets, in streets, in houses, even in the mosque. Many of the dead had been killed execution-style, with their hands tied behind their backs. Some also had stab wounds in their throats. In some cases heads had been almost entirely severed. I saw bodies that were burned black, with flesh peeling off to reveal brittle, charred skeletons. When we tried to remove the corpses to bury them, the bones crumbled in our hands. Moadamiya lost over one hundred dead in the *Shabiha*'s two-day rampage, and a far larger number remain missing.

In the aftermath of the massacre, it seemed as if all of Moadamiya was preparing to take up arms. Friends of mine who had long supported armed resistance searched for new sources of weapons. Those who wished to keep the revolution peaceful still pressed their case, but their calls for non-violent protests fell on increasingly deaf ears.

In March 2012 the regime invaded Moadamiya again, and this time I was there when it happened. It was devastating. I had been visiting our half-destroyed family apartment to pick up some clothes. Although it was uninhabitable, many of our family belongings remained, and I often found myself back there. A loud rumbling drew my attention to the window, and I walked over to see armoured personnel carriers rolling through the streets disgorging soldiers who disappeared into buildings, no doubt making their way to the rooftops. I could hear what sounded like intensive shooting and shelling in the town centre, but I could not call my friends to warn them because all electricity and communications had been cut. For three days I stayed holed up in my apartment and tried to avoid attracting attention. At night I could hear the soldiers below, drinking and singing songs about Assad, and occasionally firing into the sky. I was terrified to leave, but on the fourth day I ran out of food and was forced to venture outside.

My apartment building had been transformed into a garrison. Soldiers were roaming the halls, sitting in the lobby and milling around near their vehicles on the street below. Trying to be as nonchalant as possible, I approached a group of them and said that I was a resident of the building and that I wanted to go outside to buy food. They were polite; I can only imagine they thought I was a friend of some of the officers who still lived on this side of the railway line. They allowed me to walk to a shop across the street, which, although largely looted, still had some boxes of eggs and noodles for sale. I grabbed the items and took them to the checkout, but the soldiers refused to accept payment and 'gave' me the items. Laws no longer applied to these men.

On the fifth day of the occupation dozens of cars and minivans drove past my building with their windows open, blaring pro-Assad songs. Plain-clothes security agents, many of them with muscular physiques, poured out of these cars and began dancing in the streets, chanting, 'Our souls and our blood are yours, Bashar!' and, '*Shabiha* for ever!' The *Shabiha* had arrived. I knew then that another massacre was about to begin.

The *Shabiha* rampaged through Moadamiya for five whole days, and this time the massacre was far bloodier. When they left, I saw people gathering pieces of flesh into plastic bags without any idea to whom the parts belonged. I also remember seeing intestines draped over an olive tree. The Moadamiya local council has an office that keeps track of martyrs and missing persons from the town. In total, the office has documented some 1,400 deaths in the town since the start of the revolution. Of these, roughly a third – 450 people – died in the five days of the second *Shabiha* massacre. About 4,000 Moadamiya residents have also disappeared since March 2011, and the vast majority of them went missing during the massacres of February and March 2012.

After this second massacre, preparations for an armed uprising escalated. Residents borrowed money, sold their jewellery and obtained donations from whomever was willing to give in order to buy weapons. The number of FSA fighters in Moadamiya tripled, and ambushes of regime patrols became more numerous and more deadly. The residents even created a makeshift weapons factory, run by an trainee architect named Abu Adnan, to produce explosive anti-tank charges, which were set at key entry points around Moadamiya.

My childhood home became part of the front line. Clashes between the Free Syrian Army and Assad's men became a regular occurrence on my block. Mortars, heavy machine-gun fire and sniper rounds frequently criss-crossed the street next to my house. I had to sprint across that street to get around my neighbourhood, and on multiple occasions sniper bullets passed within metres of me as I ran.

Night was more dangerous than day. Residents who ventured outside at night were sitting ducks for the regime's snipers, because the Iranians had supplied Assad's men with rifles mounting thermal sights. Some residents tried jumping from rooftop to rooftop in order to evade the snipers on our street, but this only exposed them to snipers watching other locations. Each time I opened my apartment window at least a few bullets whizzed by my head. Lighting a cigarette or turning on a cellphone at night was tantamount to committing suicide.

I began to think about joining the fighting, and in April 2012 I and some like-minded friends drove north towards Homs, then the capital of the Syrian revolution, to take up arms, but as we were attempting to negotiate a checkpoint outside Homs, our car was shot at. To make capture more difficult, and in line with a pre-agreed plan, each of us sprinted away in a different direction to confuse the *Shabiha*. I was able to escape safely but ended up in Lebanon, and I never learned the fate of my friends. To this day I feel such guilt.

I had no money and no contacts in Lebanon, and because the Lebanese security services were harassing Syrians, I tried my best to keep a low profile. I slept in public places, performed odd jobs here and there, and managed to earn myself just enough money for the most basic necessities. I found a place to sleep with some other Syrians inside a workshop, but the only place left was the attic, which was sweltering. Within two months I was sick of the precarious refugee life.

When my family found out that I was returning to Syria, my brothers insisted that I take shelter with them in Mezze. While I was there, my mother in Jordan and my brother Yazid in England called to entreat me not to return to Moadamiya, but I faced a clear choice. If I stayed in Mezze, I would be safer, yes, but I would also have to abandon my principles and adopt the appearance of a *Shabiha* lifestyle, like my brothers. I would have to put up pictures of Assad on my wall, endure Assad's blood-red flag greeting me when I opened my cellphone, attend compulsory rallies, participate in fake elections and live in constant fear that I would say the wrong thing and be sent to a torture cell to die. I couldn't do it.

One evening I excused myself from the dinner table, pretending that I was going to the bathroom or stepping out for a smoke, but instead of doing either of these things I simply left and made my way to the nearest bus stop. By the time my brothers even realized that I had gone, I was already on a bus and well beyond their reach. I got off the bus at the Officers' Residence, which was the last regime-controlled area between Damascus and Moadamiya. In order to reach Moadamiya, I would need to pass through the Officers' Residence and cross the railroad tracks without raising suspicion.

Two Alawite guards appeared as I approached the Residence. I had no idea who they were, but I smiled, laughed and pretended that I knew them. They laughed, smiled back and let me pass without a second thought. Once inside, I made my way to the railway line. Once there I noticed a familiar face eyeing me suspiciously – one of the guards. I flashed back to the early days of the pro-democracy protests, when my friends and I would have heated discussions about the future of Syria. There had been one Alawite in particular who had been so against the protesters that I had cut off all ties with him. On one occasion, I now remembered, I had seen him walk into a restaurant with the *Shabiha* who was now squinting at me.

I veered towards him, made eye contact and struck up a conversation. I reminded him we had a mutual friend and said I had left my ID papers at his house and was just heading over to pick them up. I'd been called up for military service. He looked back at me blankly, and I asked him if he could cover me while I crossed the tracks. He was sceptical and asked if I was sure I wanted to risk it – the terrorists were shooting at everything that moved. By terrorists, he meant us – the Assad opposition. I argued back and eventually he agreed to cover me. I am almost certain that this *Shabiha* knew who I was, that he did not believe a word I was saying and only let me pass because he assumed that the 'terrorists' of Moadamiya would shoot me anyway.

I walked past him to the edge of the Officers' Residence and peered across the railroad tracks, then dashed across. The rebel lookouts held their fire, and I was back in Moadamiya.

My town had changed radically. When I returned to Moadamiya in June 2012, it was a true war zone: bombs, shelling and checkpoints were ubiquitous, the power was always out, and tanks seemed to be parked at every corner. Many more residents had fled, and those who remained spoke either of preparing to flee or of fighting on until victory. Those who still advocated peace were largely ignored; the regime had killed far too many people for that to remain a real option. A number of my friends had taken up arms and were now full-time fighters with the FSA.

After my earlier determination to fight, I had been rethinking my contribution to the movement. There were many fighters in the area now, more fighters than there were weapons. Since I was one of the few English speakers in Moadamiya, I felt I would be more useful working with the media, trying to spread the story of what was happening to us to the outside world. One of my close friends, my former neighbour Wassed, was one of the first protest organizers. In the early stages of the movement he had started a Facebook page, where he would post about the regime and its atrocities, and he then created a role for himself as communications leader.

We saw each other often; he was one of the protesters I would hide in my family home after street protests. As the fighting intensified, we had kept in touch. He knew that I had a good command of English and eventually asked me to help with translations for the Moadamiya local council. I would translate international news reports and speeches by world leaders into Arabic, translate the council media office news reports into English, and help activists in nearby towns to translate their reports into English as well. My role grew from there. I filmed FSA fighters in action when I brought food up to the front line and also documented the civilian casualties of the regime bombardments. I owned no cellphone, no camera and no computer, so I was only able to work when I was able to borrow a camera and then a laptop to upload the videos.

On my return I had relocated to a slightly safer area two blocks from where I grew up, although the escalating fighting rendered the whole district increasingly unsafe. Eventually I had to leave my old neighbourhood entirely. With a bare minimum of clothing and some essential documents, I moved to the town centre to stay with friends.

In July 2012, under a month after my return to Moadamiya, FSA formations from Moadamiya, Daraya and southern Damascus overwhelmed the regime's checkpoints and pushed into the capital city itself. These were some of the best days of the Syrian revolution. We believed that we would soon unseat Assad, end the war, free all the regime's prisoners and rebuild Syria as a democracy. Rumours circulated of an imminent battle for Damascus in which Free Syrian Army fighters from around the country would converge to capture the Syrian capital.

FSA fighters were able to advance to the Midan district of Damascus, one neighbourhood away from the crucial regime nerve centres of Mezze and Kafr Sousa, before Assad deployed overwhelming aerial firepower against them. Like angry hornets, military helicopters swarmed across the skies and rained down their deadly venom of rockets and bombs. Whole blocks within Midan were razed to the ground, and the FSA was eventually forced to retreat. Friends who had participated in the offensive vowed to try again, but only after they had obtained sufficient firepower to break through the regime's defences. That firepower never came.

As the Free Syrian Army in Moadamiya continued to press home its attacks, the regime undertook a systematic campaign to destroy the essentials of daily life in the town. Air strikes, tank incursions and artillery bombardments targeted power lines and cellphone towers, leaving tens of thousands of people dependent on makeshift electrical generators for power and communications. Only three weeks after we took over the three state hospitals in Moadamiya, precision air strikes brought them crashing to the ground, forcing us to switch to underground field hospitals with only the most basic equipment.

Sometimes regime jets would bomb evacuated streets or abandoned lots, and we would breathe a sigh of relief, but if we saw water gushing up from the site of the strike, our relief would turn to despair; this meant that a water main had been hit. From mid-2012 the entire town relied on a single damaged pipe for water, and this would probably have been targeted if it had not also served a nearby pro-regime area. Most homes in Moadamiya had water tanks that relied on electric pumps to raise water from the ground-level mains pipes, so when the power failed, so did the pumps. You could pay for a tanker truck to fill your tank, but this was expensive, and as the fighting went on became increasingly difficult. We stopped showering every day, stopped washing our clothes. Most households restricted themselves to one bathing day a week. Moving from house to house, I tried to time my arrival at a new apartment with their washing day and managed to keep relatively clean.

Assad's men still tried to recapture Moadamiya from time to time, entering in dozens, always equipped with newer and deadlier weapons, but the FSA were able to push them back and inflict massive casualties time and again. Slowly but surely, the war against Bashar al-Assad was turning into a stalemate: the regime was unable to crush the revolution in Moadamiya, but the revolution was unable to break through the regime's defences around Damascus.

In the second half of 2012, the regime changed its strategy. It pulled its forces back and contented itself with bombarding the civilians of Moadamiya from a distance. Warplanes periodically swooped down to strike houses and civilians at random, but this was more to ensure that we never felt safe rather than a coordinated campaign.

At this stage there were around 15,000 people living in Moadamiya; around three-quarters of the residents had fled. Those who were left fell into distinct categories: families who were too afraid to leave or had nowhere else to go; people who existed in a grey zone, neither supporting the regime nor part of the resistance, who refused to leave and lose everything for a conflict they felt they had no part in; those who benefited from the conflict

– warlords we called them – who had connections on both sides, profited from supplying goods ranging from food and medicine to weapons, and smuggled out civilians who wanted to leave the city; and the resistance – a surprisingly small number. I would say there were about 300 of us, although the Free Syrian Army wouldn't admit to such a low number, partly to keep up morale but also to attract money from overseas supporters.

Starvation was the main tactic in the regime's new strategy and it proved to be their most effective weapon. Although the government forces had already closed all the usual ways into Moadamiya, until now we had been able to use back roads, paths through the west Moadamiya olive groves and routes through neighbouring Daraya. In the second half of 2012, however, the regime made a concerted effort to ensure that all of these smuggling routes were closed.

Living conditions in Moadamiya deteriorated dramatically as the regime tightened the siege. Basic cooking supplies such as bread and sugar ran out. Perishable items like meat and eggs turned into near-impossible luxuries in the absence of refrigeration, and we were forced to survive on stores of non-perishable grain products such as rice, spaghetti, bulgur wheat and lentils. After a while, when these supplies dwindled as well, our situation became truly dire: we picked the leaves off the trees, pulled grass up from the ground, dug through rubbish heaps, scoured abandoned houses.

My friends and I spent much of the end of 2012 trying to bribe the *Shabiha* into breaking their own siege. We would approach their checkpoints, shout out exorbitant offers for food from a safe distance and hope that they were corrupt enough to accept. They often were. Depending on their mood, they would ask for five to ten times the normal market price for food, medical products or baby formula. Sometimes they didn't give us what we had asked for. They gave us lentils when we had paid for rice, a loaf of bread covered in mould, or baby formula past its sell-by date. But no matter how much they cheated us, we had no choice but to accept; our only alternative was to eat olives, leaves or grass.

Sometimes I would try to bribe Alawite friends from school by calling them on their cellphones. This was rarely effective; the *Shabiha* who knew me personally were even more aggressive and cruel than the checkpoint thugs. One friend I had known since the fifth grade, Wissam, had owned an electronics shop only a couple of blocks from my house. Before the revolution I would regularly visit his store to look at his stock and make small talk, but when I called him on his cellphone during the siege, he snarled at me, saying I would be on my knees before long. I cursed him and hung up. What made him hate me, hate the town, hate his own people so much?

By the end of 2012, desperate conditions had begun to cloud the thinking of the residents of Moadamiya. The regime rotated fresh troops into Moadamiya to replace the old checkpoint *Shabiha*. Rumours circulated that their commander was an Iranian general, and we did not recognize a single face among our new besiegers. The Iranians were supporting Assad, supplying weapons and Lebanese Hezbollah fighters skilled in urban warfare. Worse yet, the new troops refused to smuggle food into Moadamiya, no matter how much money we offered them. From December 2012 the ordinary residents in Moadamiya had virtually no access to the food, medicine and other supplies they needed to survive.

Some residents became atheists, saying that God could never have abandoned them to such a fate; others compared the siege to one described in the Quran. In the seventh year of the Prophet Muhammad the leaders of Mecca began a siege of his tribe that lasted for three years, during which many thousands died. The siege was only lifted because some of the leaders felt ashamed of starving their own people. As I have said, other residents abandoned all semblance of morality, becoming hoarders of food and medicine. Attempts were made to crack down on the warlords, but there was little the council could do because they had their own private militias. The town began to turn on itself, but no one in Moadamiya could have imagined what was to come.

Events were about to take a much darker turn, leading to the moment when I would first pick up a weapon and fight: 21 August 2013 would change me for ever.

Chemical Day
21 August 2013

4.15 a.m.–6.30 a.m.

My eyes were burning, my head was throbbing and my throat was rasping for air. I was suffocating.

I tried my best to inhale – once, twice, three times. All I heard was that same horrible scraping sound as my throat blocked. The drumming pain in my head became unbearable. The world began to blur

Suddenly my windpipe opened again. The air ripped through my throat and pierced my lungs. Invisible needles stabbed my eyes. A searing pain clawed at my stomach. I doubled over and shouted to my roommates, 'Wake up! It's a chemical attack!'

Abu Abdo, my high school writing partner; Ahmad, a friend from middle school; and Alm Dar, a Free Syrian Army field commander, scrambled out of their beds in panic. I rushed to the bathroom and slapped water all over my face. I heard a din outside – screams from my neighbours.

My friends were also fighting for breath and coughing with all their force. We staggered around the room, panting and retching as we tried to put on our clothes as quickly as possible. Even before we could finish, we heard rapid and urgent bangs at the door. Ahmad ran to open it.

It was our neighbour Um Khaled. 'Help, please, they're dying,' she gasped. She was carrying her children, four and six, one under each arm. Both were unconscious. Their faces were blue and yellow and they were vomiting an ugly white froth from their mouths.

Alm Dar ran downstairs to get his old white truck. Ahmad and Abu Abdo picked up the children and followed. I raced through the building to make sure no one else was hurt.

I hurried downstairs to the street, rushing past blasted-out windows, crumbling walls, pockmarked floors and piles of rubble. When I reached the front door and looked outside, I stopped short and stared in terror.

Dozens of men, women and children were writhing in pain on the ground. Other people were shouting for doctors, praying and calling to Allah in the heavens, pleading for their fallen loved ones to start breathing again.

Out of the corner of my eye, I noticed a large lump lying in the dirt about fifty metres to my left. As I moved closer, I realized that it was a small boy with his face to the ground. I ran to turn him over.

The sight of his face made me forget every horror I had seen in the past three years: the burned and rotting corpses after massacres, the woman and children shredded into pieces by shelling, the cries of my friends as they lay wounded from combat – I forgot them all. All I could focus on was the innocent face of this boy stained with grotesque shades of red, yellow and blue. His eyes returned an empty, glassy stare. White vomit oozed from his mouth, and a grating sound rasped from his throat as he struggled to breathe.

I took off his shirt and tried to blow air into his mouth. I pressed his chest and tried to pump the white poison from his lungs. I screamed for help, begged Allah for mercy. None of it helped.

After two or three minutes Alm Dar pulled up in a truck overflowing with injured women and children. He stared blankly at the boy, turned to his overflowing truck, turned back to me. I sat in the back with the boy. He was still struggling to breathe, that horrible grating sound still coming from his throat. We drove past more bodies and wailing survivors. I held him and cried.

When we pulled into the field hospital, I lifted the boy down. He seemed heavier than before. I could barely keep my balance and had to use all my strength to lay him on the ground. Then the world began to shimmer and turn grey, and the ground rose up to meet me.

I woke to find a man holding me and yelling that I was alive. He had a long wet black beard and red-brown eyes. I knew him: Ahmad. My friend, my housemate, Ahmad.

I looked around. I was in a building – no, a basement, with only small high windows to the outside. There was no electrical power, only a few candles, flashlights and dim rays of sunlight creeping in through the windows. All around me people were crying, wailing, throwing water on bodies, giving injections and pumping chests. The floor was wet and cold and covered with blood.

Three men approached, two carrying buckets of water and one holding a syringe. The two men splashed water across my body as the doctor injected me with a clear liquid. I was in great pain, but as the liquid coursed through me,

I began to feel stronger. I tried to push the men back when they bent down to pick me up. 'Let's go upstairs,' they told me. 'The air is starting to get poisoned in here.'

They helped me up a set of broken, rusty stairs into the open air. I shielded my face as a red ray of sunlight hit my eyes. It was morning, and the sun was rising. All around me people were crying, trying to revive their friends and relatives.

I took a few steps to a burned-out bus in the middle of the street. The bus seemed familiar; I had a clear memory of seeing it on fire. I stopped and looked around. I knew this place. I'd been here before. This was the field hospital in Moadamiya. People ran over and hugged me. 'Praise Allah, you're alive! Kassem, you're alive!'

I began to recognize my friends and neighbours. Here was Mouawia, my next-door neighbour; here was Ahmad, Abu Abdo and Abu Malek, my football buddy since seventh grade. The people I had grown up with, in what seemed like aeons ago.

But I still couldn't understand what had happened to me. Why did I feel so cold? I looked down at my body and realized that I was wearing only my boxer shorts.

'Where are my clothes?' I asked.

'We can't bring you your clothes, brother,' said Abu Malek. 'They're covered in water and sarin. Assad hit us with sarin gas.' He left to get me something to wear.

The past few hours came flooding back to me. I remembered gasping for air, inhaling the most painful breath of my life. I recalled running to the street, seeing bodies everywhere, and the horrible, glassy stare of that little boy.

Abu Malek returned with a jacket and a blanket. 'Now you should be—'

A huge explosion shook the ground and swallowed the rest of his sentence. More explosions followed in rapid succession around us: tank shells, mortars, heavy artillery, missiles and other weapons I didn't recognize. A desperate effort to evacuate the hospital began. A group of Free Syrian Army fighters sprinted past me. Abu Jabal, a young fighter I knew, urged everyone to take cover, to fight. His pale face turned red as he yelled louder and louder. His wet brown beard bobbed up and down. I stared at him, rooted to the ground.

I heard a distant roar overhead: Assad's warplanes were approaching. I craned my neck towards the sky, watching for them and waiting for the sound of bombs. Was this really happening? I looked in all directions, surveying the ruins of my neighbourhood, searching for something, anything that would help me make sense of it.

Alm Dar was shouting to get my attention. I listened and stared but did not reply. I just couldn't process what was happening. He slapped me across the face.

'Are they trying to invade?' I asked dumbly.

'Yes!'

'From where?'

'Everywhere! We need everyone at the front lines. Can you fight?'

'Yes.'

In truth, I had never fought before.

He helped me into his truck. I still don't know how we made it to his headquarters, with bombs falling around us in every direction. When we arrived I went into a bathroom and splashed myself with water. Someone knocked on the door and handed me pyjama trousers and a T-shirt. I put the clothes on and returned to the sink to try to wash the burning sensation out of my eyes, but I couldn't recognize the reflection in the mirror. Whoever – or whatever – this was, it was not Kassem. This was a monster, a beast, with bloodshot eyes and a wild face contorted with fury and pain, an image of anger personified.

I had never before wanted to be a fighter, but in that moment of my life it was all I wanted to be.

8.30 a.m.–12.00 p.m.

I left the bathroom. At this point I had stopped caring whether anything made sense or not, whether I lived or died. I was given a protective vest and an AK-47. I didn't know how to use the rifle, but I headed outside, intending to find the front line.

Alm Dar ran to catch up with me. 'Kassem, wait! We have to do this as a team. Give everyone else time to get ready, and then we'll move out together.'

I was electric with adrenaline but agreed to do as he said. Alm Dar walked me back to his base and outlined our task. We were to defend four crucial blocks in north-eastern Moadamiya, near Highway 40, which ran straight into the heart of Damascus. First though we would need to sprint through an open area, dodging sniper fire. He told me how to use the gun and handed me a grenade.

When everyone was ready, we stood together and looked at each other. There were about thirty of us. I studied each face carefully – friends, neighbours, people I had grown up with who I might never see again. Together we shouted, 'Allahu akbar' – God is greatest – in the desperate hope that he would hear our prayers.

We moved along the planned route. Eventually we came to an area where there was no cover and huddled in a dark stairwell, listening to the mortars and artillery shells above us. The explosions never stopped, but we began to make out a rhythm to the maelstrom. At times the bombardment was so heavy that the explosions seemed to merge into one big crackling sound. At other times we were able to make out individual explosions. We waited for just such a lull, and then Alm Dar flicked his wrist. We charged on to the street and added our voices to the cacophony. Abu Jabal punctuated our cries with sporadic bursts of covering fire from his heavy machine gun.

It took us ten seconds to reach our target building, but it felt more like ten years. I heard bullets whizz within inches of my head. I heard the plaintive shriek of heavy mortar bombs as they dived towards the ground. With the burn of the sarin still stinging my eyes, and dust stirred up from the bombardment swirling in the air, I could barely even see our destination. We reached the centre of the road – the most exposed location. A mortar shell screamed into a balcony above me, exploding in a red flash and raining dust and rubble on to the ground to my right. Civilians ran frantically past, some rushing to their homes, some fleeing their homes, and some just running out of sheer panic. I should have been terrified, but I was not. I was existing on pure adrenaline, and my anger was stronger than my fear. I felt a strange sense of power, as if I could eat tanks and spit fire.

We reached the target building. Darting around a wall, we moved out of the enemy's line of sight and dashed through an open doorway into the building's dark interior. We gathered – there seemed to be fewer of us than when we had started – and Alm Dar sent some fighters to the basement before motioning for the rest of us to follow him down the hall.

He charged into the first room and swung his gun in all directions. Then he turned, shouted 'Clear!' and motioned for us to check the other rooms. Since I had never fought before, I tried to copy Alm Dar as best I could. I lunged into the next open room, pointed my gun at each corner and kept my finger tight on the trigger to shoot at even the slightest movement. When all the rooms were clear, we gathered again and took up firing positions. With a man called Ahmad I was stationed in a second-floor room that overlooked the local mosque. We were to watch the street and shoot any regime troops that tried to pass through the crossroads.

We heard the metallic roar of the tanks before we saw them: four huge beasts of iron and steel. FSA fighters ran into the road and fired directly at the tanks with machine guns. This barely dented their armour, and when the tanks returned fire, the fighters retreated into alleys. I wondered what they were trying to do, but then I heard a series of deafening explosions. Two tanks flew into the air and landed on their sides. It had been a ruse; the FSA fighters had been drawing the tanks towards explosive devices.

I had watched my friend Abu Adnan, who had been an architect in training before the war, build explosive devices in a makeshift weapons factory in Moadamiya, and I had heard the stories of FSA fighters who had given their lives planting his handiwork on the front lines. This was an extremely dangerous job, as they could be killed by regime snipers or even friendly fire, or, if they were very unlucky, the devices themselves could be accidentally triggered. But now two Assad tanks had been destroyed, and the other two were cautiously backing away. Though mortar bombs still crashed into the ground and heavy machine-gun bullets still ripped through the walls of the building, I felt a strange sense of calm, as if the bombardment had somehow lightened.

The next thing I remember is a blinding flash of red light, and then I was hurled backwards through the air. The world turned black. I could not tell if I was dead or alive. Fire, rubble and flaming shrapnel flew past me, but I felt none of it.

My face began to hurt, followed by my back, my eyes, my lungs. Everything hurt.

I heard a voice: 'Kassem! Open your eyes! Are you all right?'

I opened my eyes slowly and cautiously. The first thing I saw was sunlight, then clouds of dust, and then a long, dusty black beard bobbing up and down. Ahmad was shouting at me. The building had been hit, but somehow I had managed to avoid serious injury. I asked for a cigarette, took a few quick puffs and returned to my firing position.

A few minutes later Assad troops appeared. They looked like special forces of some kind and were dressed in full chemical gear. They were lumbering towards an alley between two houses. Without thinking, I swept my AK-47 from side to side and pressed the trigger. I then realized that my gun was on semi-automatic, so I switched to full automatic and emptied the magazine in under a minute. Men collapsed to the ground. I scrambled to load another magazine and waited for more soldiers to appear. None did.

I realized then that I had just killed another human being. Not just one. I felt a surge of confused emotions. I couldn't tell whether I was proud or sad. It felt like I had been walking for days under a hot desert sun dying from thirst, and when I finally drank what I thought was water, it turned out to be sand and scorched my parched throat. I had ended someone's life, a person who had had a family, friends, a name, a birthday. Now they no longer existed.

Though the shelling continued, the battle's deadly symphony seemed to be winding down. Hearing shouts from the rooftop, we ran up and looked out to see what looked like the 4th Division making a hasty retreat. Another fighter ran up to us with a radio; we could hear their distress calls.

'Did you hack into their channels?'

'No,' he replied. 'We retrieved the radio from one of the soldiers we killed.'

He kicked some rubble and shook his fist, emptied his machine-gun clip at some random dust piles, then ordered us off the rooftop.

Even though the battle was over, I returned to my firing position. I sat down on a plastic chair, lit a cigarette and replayed the day's events in my head. My hands were shaking. Everything seemed so surreal. I looked out at the ruins of Moadamiya, but I didn't feel anything, couldn't make sense of anything.

I blacked out again.

Damn humanity
21 August–10 September 2013

Dim lights, wailing women and the disgusting scent of blood and antiseptic – I was back in the field hospital. I opened my eyes to the sight of a nurse manually pumping air into my mouth.

I later found out that I'd stopped breathing, and the doctors had to give me more atropine and CPR. Two men then took me to a nearby friend's house. I saw four friends of mine lying on the floor, so I lay down next to them and drifted off to sleep. It was daybreak when I woke again. I was still in pain, mainly from my chest, and my breathing was difficult. My eyes were raw. I could make out my friends still sleeping around me and a nurse sitting on a chair facing towards us. I got up. The only thing I could think to do was to splash myself with water, try to clean myself up a little and clear my head. I thanked the woman for taking care of me and went outside.

Assad's forces had resumed the bombardment of Moadamiya, so my thoughts turned back to the front lines. I tuned out the thunderous explosions of Assad's shelling and quelled the angry rumblings in my empty stomach. I prayed.

I was determined to keep fighting, still running on adrenaline, and made my way to the farmlands and olive groves of west Moadamiya, where a Free Syrian Army leader named Murad had set up his headquarters. I offered my help, and he gave me a weapon – an M4 assault rifle – something I'd only ever seen in computer games. I then headed towards the north-eastern front.

Alm Dar flashed the victory sign when he saw me. I went to his headquarters, where I picked out a protective vest and more ammunition – each of the leaders had different sets of weapons and protective gear. Then Abu Jabal, one of the top FSA commanders in Moadamiya, gathered all the fighters at the front together to explain our mission. We needed to push Assad's troops back. If they were able to keep the areas they had gained they would bring up reinforcements, and we'd be at risk of losing the whole northern sector of the city.

We advanced, shouting prayers as we ran, spraying bullets and lobbing grenades towards the enemy in an effort to cover our move. Regime forces replied with a hail of gunfire and mortars. We reached the first building. One fighter hammered a hole in the wall with a pickaxe, a second hurled six grenades through the hole, and a third opened fire with his heavy machine gun. Then we all leaped into the building, running past the soldiers we had just killed. As we proceeded to the next building, Abu Jabal grabbed my shoulder, instructing me to cover our advance with the snipers. Suddenly a tank shell slammed into the wall next to me and threw me to the ground. Rubble from the impact rained down on to my head. I brushed the dust from my eyes, lifted my head. I heard another thunderous explosion, and the tank went flying. Another anti-tank device had saved us.

It took us under three hours to recapture all of our lost territory. By three that afternoon Assad's forces had retreated entirely.

After the fighting stopped, I lost consciousness yet again, only to wake hours later in a field hospital. My friend Waseem came over with a cellphone – my mother had been trying to contact me. I phoned her and reassured her I was fine. She was crying, but I had to go. I tried to say goodbye as casually as possible, even though I knew that I might never hear her voice again, and I hung up overwhelmed with emotion.

I wandered through the streets instead of sleeping that night. I finally took refuge under an olive tree deep in the groves of west Moadamiya. The pale white moonlight streaked in between the leaves and into my burning eyes. I had never felt so lonely. I was desperate for a hug, but all the people I wanted to hug were beyond my reach. I wept, then, after looking around to make sure that I was really alone, I hugged the olive tree. 'There's no one else left to hug,' I told it. 'I used to play on you as a boy and eat your fruit. My baba, my mama, my brothers and all my friends were there. Do you remember those days? We used to have such fun. Now everyone is gone, and only you are left.'

A faint breeze stroked the leaves across my face. I closed my eyes and imagined that someone was wiping my tears away, then I had the strong feeling that I was in fact being watched. I resumed my wanderings and after a while found myself in the ruins of my family's apartment. The front door was broken in, the walls were pockmarked with bullet holes, the windows shattered, and our furniture lay in pieces on the floor.

I sifted through the wreckage and found my old football shirt. I pressed it tight to my chest. As I made my way through my home, I thought about the many hours I had spent there with my family and friends. I could hardly believe that my old life had been real. The sight of our broken TV drew my attention and took me back to the many hours of uneven black-and-white images I had viewed on the screen. After my father passed away Thursday night became movie night for the entire family. A different family member would pick a movie each week, and there would be popcorn, snacks and a big pot of sweet tea as we watched. This was our way of trying to bring back a small portion of the joy that we had lost for ever when my father died.

The first few rays of sunlight crept across the horizon. I needed to leave. I raced through the early-morning prayer and said goodbye to my home. I recited the Martyrs' Prayer before dashing on to the street as sniper bullets zoomed past me. Before everything began I hadn't been sure if I truly believed in God, but I was sure now. There was no other possible explanation for why I was still alive, and if I wasn't sure that there would be divine justice, that these people would face retribution in the next life, how could I have gone on? This was all I had.

Later I would learn that United Nations chemical inspectors had been at the hotel I used to work at in Damascus when Bashar al-Assad hit us with sarin. I would also discover that at least 1,500 people perished during the 21 August 2013 sarin gas attacks, which targeted the eastern Ghouta suburbs of Damascus and Moadamiya. I lost many close friends and neighbours in the attacks. Informants inside the regime later told me that, as Assad's rockets were flying through the air, the regime's defence secretary and the governor of Damascus were at the Mezze military airbase waiting to declare the targeted areas 'liberated from terrorists' in front of state TV cameras.

On 26 August 2013, at approximately 11 a.m., UN chemical weapons inspectors arrived at the eastern entrance of Moadamiya after days of intense international pressure to investigate the attacks. The 4th Division attempted to detain the inspectors at its checkpoints, warning them that al-Qaeda was waiting inside, but the inspectors were undeterred. At around 1.30 p.m. Assad's officers ran out of excuses, and the inspectors entered Moadamiya to begin their investigations.

The inspectors entered Moadamiya in four UN vehicles each carrying around twelve passengers, most of them Europeans. Free Syrian Army fighters accompanied the inspectors at all times. We escorted the inspectors to the field hospital, where they examined victims and took blood and tissue samples, and we escorted them to the missile impact sites, where they performed many tests and took pages of notes in evidence. At around 4.30 p.m. the regime warned that it was 'no longer responsible for the safety' of the inspectors, and they were forced to depart. As soon as the inspectors cleared Assad's checkpoints, the 4th Division resumed its attacks.

I took shelter from the bombardment in my friend Waseem's house. He had been trying to call me all day; he had received a call from a BBC World reporter who wanted to interview me after seeing me speak in English on a live stream. Only minutes before my first media interview began, Waseem advised me to use a pseudonym to protect myself and my family. I chose the first two names that popped into my head: Qusai, after the popular Syrian TV actor Qusai Kuli, and Zakarya, which was the first name of an uncle of mine in Jordan. Qusai Zakarya would become my persona for all things connected with the Syrian revolution.

Within minutes of the interview, my phone erupted with Skype messages and friending requests from reporters around the world. Over the next two weeks I only slept a few hours each night due to the number of news interviews I was giving and the different time zones the reporters called from. I spent all of my time either speaking to reporters or trying to recharge my phone – and recharging a phone battery was a tall order because there were only a few makeshift electrical generators (powered by olive oil and nail polish remover) in all of Moadamiya. But despite my fatigue, stress and hunger, and despite the lingering burn of sarin in my eyes, I never turned down an interview request. I hoped that my testimony would make a difference and help bring an end to the brutal siege of my town.

Two weeks after the chemical attacks we received an unexpected hammer blow: Barack Obama, who had previously declared Assad's use of chemical weapons to be a 'red line', announced that he would ask the US Congress for approval before initiating a military strike. When I first heard Obama vow to strike Assad, when he declared in soaring rhetoric that the US would not look away from the atrocities of tyrants, I had shed tears of joy. I believed then that the United States of America, the land of the free, was finally coming to the aid of Syrians just as it had come to the aid of so many other peoples seeking freedom. But the minute I heard Obama announce that he would seek the consent of Congress, I began to doubt.

We waited for the world to give its verdict on the importance of our suffering, the value of our lives. Obama consulted Congress, the British parliament debated, and the French prevaricated. I tried to stay optimistic, telling myself that Congress might give Obama permission for an even bigger strike than he had requested, but deep down I knew the truth. On 14 September 2013 Obama struck a deal with Russia that allowed Assad to escape punishment for his crimes as long as he gave up his chemical weapons stockpile. Even though Assad had just gassed hundreds of women and children to death, he would be able to continue bombing and starving us without punishment.

I watched the announcement on a live feed in my friend's basement alongside others sheltering from the ongoing bombardment. I was translating Obama's speech into Arabic in real time, but I stopped when Obama announced the deal. I didn't have the heart to look my friends in the eye and tell them that the United States had caved in and that Bashar al-Assad had won again. Instead I ran into the street, ignoring the explosions, and I started crying, cursing, screaming and kicking everything in my way. A number of people had to restrain me before I was finally able to share the horrible news.

It turned out that Assad had been very smart – by hitting us with sarin while UN inspectors were in Damascus. He gained himself a year of immunity from international pressure that he could use to starve us while his chemical stocks were being removed. He exposed the sermons about shared humanity as lies and proved that, when confronted with obvious and unspeakable evil, the world will do everything in its power to look away.

In times of war or natural disaster hope is priceless. It can make up for low ammunition, food shortages, stress, fatigue and almost any physical ailment. Hope is the fuel of hearts and souls. Until the moment Obama announced his deal with Russia, I and my friends had hoped that humankind would come to our aid. Afterwards I gave up on humanity. There is nothing – nothing – worse than feeling the world has forgotten you.

Walled in
August–November 2013

The world's attention drifted away from Moadamiya after the September 2013 chemical deal, but death did not. A new murderer, starvation, was Assad's latest tool, and the most vulnerable residents – women, children, the old and the wounded – were the first to succumb. Slowly starvation clouded their eyesight, gnawed at their bodies and drained them of hope.

The situation in Moadamiya was dire, but it was not unique. The town was suffering alongside dozens of others across Syria as part of the regime's plan to bring Syrians to their knees. Moadamiya was however geopolitically significant. It was considered the western gateway to Damascus and surrounded by Assad's most powerful and loyal military assets: in the east the Mezze military airbase and the headquarters of Air Force Intelligence, in the north the elite 4th Division under Maher al-Assad – Bashar's brother. Leaving the town under rebel control made Assad fearful of a surprise attack on Damascus and gave the revolution hope and an example of defiance.

Assad's supporters called his new strategy Kneel or
Starve, and his supporters joked about it on pro-regime
Facebook pages: 'We should throw them a few pieces of
bread. Let them kill each other fighting for it!' 'We caught
some rats trying to sneak in food – we stuffed it down
their throats until they suffocated!'

I asked my friends in the Moadamiya media office
to film malnourished residents, interview doctors and
document the symptoms of starvation. I also called all
the reporters I knew, the reporters who had exhausted me
with their countless interview requests on chemical weapons, and asked them to cover Assad's silent massacre as it
unfolded. No one was interested; they wanted evidence
that people were dying, but I didn't understand why we
had to wait for children to die before our suffering was
worth covering. On 31 August 2013, just ten days after
Chemical Day, the world got its evidence: two-year-old
Ibraheem Khalil and seven-year-old Ammar Arafeh both
passed away from starvation. I sent videos of their final
days to every reporter I knew.

Arwa Damon and Raja Rezek of CNN were the first to
respond. Arwa presented scenes of the siege in Moadamiya,
including footage of Ibraheem's last days, to news anchor
Wolf Blitzer on CNN before asking, 'If America was able
to threaten the use of force . . . when it came to chemical weapons, well why is that same kind of pressure not
being applied to create humanitarian corridors?' I was also
contacted by the *New York Times* reporters Anna Barnard
and Muhammad Ghannam, who published an article on
starvation sieges across Syria in November 2013. Their
article began and ended with the story of an eighteen-
month-old infant from Moadamiya named Rana Obeid,
whose father was a good friend of mine. Rana was born

with food all around her. Her father had a nice house and owned a grocery shop that was renowned in Moadamiya for its yogurt. But regime bombardments took his shop and his house away from him, and one year later the regime's siege took his daughter as well. Rana needed baby formula to survive, and there was none to be had. Her father could only pray for help that never came as his daughter wasted away.

The story of Assad's starvation sieges was taken up by almost every major media outlet in the months that followed. Unlike other such deaths around the world, those in Syria were unique because they took place in a country that was food self-sufficient. Only three minutes' drive away in downtown Damascus food was plentiful, but Assad's checkpoints ensured that none of those supplies ever reached us. This made the agony of Moadamiya's residents all the more painful. As we watched our friends and family members slowly waste away, we were keenly aware that all the restaurants we knew and loved in Damascus were still operating.

The United Nations could not help. Russia, a staunch supporter of the regime, continued to use its veto in the UN Security Council to shield Assad from pressure, and the US did not push hard enough to get the veto lifted. As hopes for international action dimmed, brave and desperate residents took matters into their own hands by attempting to smuggle food, medicine and baby formula into Moadamiya past regime checkpoints. They rarely came back alive.

One night I was riding my bicycle to a friend's house when two shirtless masked men jumped out at me from the roadside. I swerved away and jumped off my bike in terror, but I then recognized the voice of an old friend from high school, Abd al-Rahman. Two years above me, Abd al-Rahman and I had played football together, and I saw him often around town. Clever with electronics, he fixed radios during the siege and was active in seeking aid. He explained that they needed help burying Abu Muhammad, a man who had been killed trying to smuggle in medicine for his daughter. For days they had tried to reach his body, but regime snipers often watched corpses, shooting anyone who tried to recover them for burial. They now had the body and there were four of them, Abd al-Rahman explained; the other two were waiting outside a nearby building. When I asked why I was needed if he already had three men to help him, he replied, 'You need to see the body.'

As we walked on, an odour so foul began to overwhelm my senses. I took my shirt off to use as a mask, but the smell seeped into my lungs. I gagged and doubled over as waves of nausea roiled my stomach. Lying in the sun, Abu Muhammad's corpse had swollen to the size of three adult males put together. He was wrapped in a white burial shroud according to Muslim custom, but the two men who had wrapped him were vomiting profusely on to the ground. Though we urged them to go, they refused to leave until Abu Muhammad was buried.

The regime had been killing civilians faster than we could dig graves. Early on, when it was still a peaceful protest movement, the regime had shot at funerals in Moadamiya's main cemetery, so two whole new grave-yards had been established in unofficial locations. But the regime soon discovered and targeted these locations as well. Tombs were reopened, corpses were pulled from their graves, and bodies had to be reburied. We had neither the time nor the resources for a fourth cemetery, so we were often forced to bury new victims on top of the old.

We opened a grave to bury Abu Muhammad, but his swollen body was too large. It took a full hour of digging before the grave was wide enough, and by this time we were tired. It took all of us to lift him, and as we shuffled towards the grave someone lost his grip and the body tumbled to the dirt. The shroud fell off, exposing Abu Muhammad's upper torso. It was swollen and discoloured into ugly shades of red, black and blue. There were cuts and cigarette burns all over his chest, and huge chunks of skin near his shoulders had melted away to the bone, as if burned by acid. His head was almost severed from his neck.

Abd al-Rahman jumped into the grave to pull the body down, and we pushed it towards him. Retching from the smell, he somehow managed to drag the body into the grave and climb out before collapsing on to the grass. I was traumatized by the sight of Abu Muhammad's body – we all were. We shovelled the earth back into the grave and I left as quickly as possible. I rode my bicycle straight to my friend Ammar's house and wept. I washed myself, but nothing seemed to remove the smell. Over the days that followed it lingered no matter how much soap I used.

The siege wore on, and many residents of Moadamiya slipped into total despair. People gave up on the world, the revolution, their families and their own lives. They stopped sheltering at home in the daylight hours, when the bombardments were at their heaviest, and they allowed their children to play outdoors even as mortar bombs were crashing down nearby.

I was not surprised when I later heard that some FSA fighters were cutting deals with the regime. These men gave up sensitive information, paid massive bribes and sometimes even surrendered in order to bring food into the town or help family members escape. Although their actions definitely hurt our cause, I am not sure if I can call them traitors. Almost every fighter in Moadamiya had lost friends or relatives, or had a sick or injured family member they were willing to do anything to save.

Even animals were affected by the crushing siege. Stray dogs began behaving like savage wolves: they ate corpses, attacked humans and each other in loud and vicious fights. Packs of dogs harassed me when I walked or biked through town at night. I started carrying a gun with me whenever I went outside just to protect myself from them.

Assad let only two items into Moadamiya during the siege: munitions and cigarettes. Most Free Syrian Army fighters were smokers, and without cigarettes those hundreds of armed Moadamiya residents might have lost their minds. To avoid this unpredictable and potentially dangerous outcome, the regime made sure that a few boxes of cigarettes periodically found their way into Moadamiya by supplying them to profiteers who sold them at astronomical prices. While before the war a single pack of cigarettes cost just a dollar, the cigarette warlords exploited and impoverished their fellow townsmen by pricing cigarettes at up to $300 a pack, but the desperate kept buying because there was no other source. There was virtually no food, and money had no real value, but cigarettes could at least offer a brief respite.

I was one of the desperate. Sometimes my richer friends took pity on me and gave me a cigarette; other times I tried to relieve my craving by rolling bizarre cigarettes made of tea leaves, dried mint, paper – almost anything that would generate smoke. I even searched through piles of rubbish in search of smokable materials. My friends and I frequently waded through rubble and garbage dumps in the hope of finding a useful or edible item. One day we found a jar of pumpkin jam that was many months past its expiration date with a layer of dirt on top of the jam. We would have been repulsed at the very sight of it before the revolution, but after months under siege, we saw only food. We scraped off the dirt and scooped the jam out of the jar with our hands. About forty minutes later, we began to feel very peaceful – we had become high by eating the rotted jam on empty stomachs. This was the best thing that had happened to us for ages – an escape from reality, a break from the agony of starvation. When we realized what had happened, we looked at that jar as if it had been filled with diamonds. We searched the town for another like it, but we were never able to find one.

Music and pop culture were more healthy forms of escape. During the siege I befriended a man named Abu Omar, who had left his medical course at a prestigious private university to join the revolution in the early days of the protests. Perhaps he did not feel that he was losing much; his ambition had been a musical career, and he had only gone down the medical route under heavy pressure from his family. His brother Saeed also joined the early protests and later became a top weapons smuggler for the FSA. When Saeed was arrested in the course of a weapons drop, a devastated Abu Omar took over his brother's trade.

I hated Abu Omar the first time I saw him. He walked into my friend's house one evening wearing headphones, shorts down to his knees, and a Colt pistol on his belt. His rusty voice sounded like nails screeching against a blackboard, and he bored me with his endless droning about weapons procurement and aid supplies. As the night wore on, I lost interest in what he was saying, so I put on my own headphones to listen to the Canadian rock band Evanescence. But then Abu Omar threw a pillow at me. He had heard the band through my headphones – he liked them too. We spent the next hour discussing our tastes in music, movies and popular culture as our friends looked on with blank stares.

We became very close after that night. During the siege Abu Omar and I would often try to forget our hunger pangs by surfing food websites and imagining how it would feel to eat again. We would also recall how well we used to eat before the revolution. I remembered how my friends and I would head to Midan, the restaurant district of downtown Damascus, where we would eat shawarma, falafel and Arab sweets like *hareesa* (sweet meat porridge) and *halawet al-jibn* (sweet cheese rolls). Those days were over, but Abu Omar and I tried our best to forget our hunger by exchanging crazy stories about how we used to stuff ourselves.

We also had fantastical debates between ourselves. I would ask him, 'If you were sentenced to spend your whole life on an island, and you could only eat sweets or regular food, which would you choose?' He gave a different answer each time depending on his mood, but my answer was always the same: 'I would choose sweets for sure. If I felt like eating something salty, I could always take a sip from the sea.'

One song that we both enjoyed was 'Wahdon' (Only They), a melancholy song by the popular Lebanese singer Fairuz. The song is about the trees of the woods and their timelessness, but under siege the song took on a whole new meaning. That song represented for me the stories of my friends who had died trying to escape the siege through the woods. Their destiny was to be swallowed up by Moadamiya's majestic olive groves, yet they lived on in the ancient memories of those towering trees.

Only they remain, like the flowers of Baylasan
They alone gather in the leaves of time
They surround and shade the forests like rain
And they knock on my doors, on my doors
Oh, long ago! The plants that have spread over these walls
Have lit up the flowers of night within my book
The dovecote is fortified and tall
The pigeons have left and I am alone, alone.

As I was listening to this song one day, Nazeer walked into the room with a weak smile on his face. I had known Nazeer since middle school. He was a very handsome guy, and he used to delight in his ability to attract women. Just before the siege began, Nazeer was about to get married, but the wedding was cancelled when his future brother-in-law was killed by regime shelling. His fiancée left Moadamiya soon afterwards with her entire family, and when Nazeer's brother was killed as well, his own family followed suit. Only Nazeer, the handsome ladies' man, was left behind to fight for Moadamiya and avenge his brothers' deaths. He braved many long months of bombardments, chemical attacks and starvation as an FSA fighter, pining all the while for his beloved fiancée. Every now and then he would ask me for romantic songs to send her.

When Nazeer walked in, he exclaimed, 'My God, Qusai, what a song! What's it called?'

'It's called "Wahdon". I'm surprised you don't remember it.'

'I can barely remember my own name now. I like it, though.'

'I think we're too old, my friend.'

Nazeer did not talk much that day. Nobody in that room did. Each of us just stared into space, peering into his memories and drowning privately in his own pain. When Nazeer left that day, he gave us all a warm goodbye. Under a week later, we heard that Nazeer had been captured and tortured to death beneath the olive trees. He had been trying to escape the siege to be reunited with his fiancée.

I was not as sad as I expected to be when I heard of Nazeer's passing. I had reached a kind of numbness. Death began to seem like a possible release, and I began to take pleasure in dancing with it. Whenever Assad's forces attacked, I would rush to the front line hoping that this battle would punch my ticket to the world beyond.

One day we got a tip that hundreds of fighters from the Lebanese militia Hezbollah were poised to attack Moadamiya alongside Assad's special forces. The plan was to attack from both the east and west, without any shelling beforehand, so as to create an element of surprise. Regime forces were set to unveil their new Russian T-80 tanks for the first time. We even learned the names of the commanding officers and the locations where they would gather their troops. Hezbollah forces were to assemble at the eastern entrance of Moadamiya, inside the Othman Mosque, while the special forces would attack from the west after massing on the former site of a large clothing store called Asia.

Almost a hundred rebel fighters, myself included, volunteered to disrupt this offensive with sneak dawn attacks. I chose to fight on the eastern front because I knew that Hezbollah had fiercer fighters and I had never faced them before. I did not want to miss this opportunity. We began our attack at 6 a.m. My job was to use my M4 rifle to pin down the enemy while FSA fighters stormed their positions on foot. My friend Abu Adnan, placed alongside me, was to help me by firing a mortar to confuse the enemy and force them to leave their shelters. I chose a spot on the third floor of a building, figuring that no one would expect fire from such a risky and exposed location.

Abu Adnan and others initiated the attack by firing a barrage of mortar bombs at Hezbollah's assembly point. Only minutes later the Hezbollah fighters ran from their cover, allowing me to begin picking them off one by one with my rifle. The regime then deployed its new tanks and bombarded us for hours, but we stood firm and managed to destroy a number of the tanks by luring them on to pre-laid explosive devices. Meanwhile, I took aim at every Hezbollah fighter I saw. I was almost out of ammunition when my adversaries finally spotted my location.

As I was sticking my gun through a hole in the balcony wall to fire at the street below, a massive bullet slammed into the wall causing it to explode in my face. I was thrown back on to the floor. By some miracle I survived the impact unscathed, but then I flew into a rage. I stood up, pushed my friends away, cursed and screamed, and dashed back to the balcony to fire my M4 wildly in the direction of the Hezbollah positions. When I had used up my ammunition, I switched to throwing lumps of rubble from the balcony until other fighters tackled me to the ground and dragged me back for my own safety.

I think I got so emotional because this incident reminded me of Adnan, a neighbour who had been one of my closest friends. Adnan was originally a friend of my younger brother Waddah, who had died suddenly and tragically one New Year's Eve. After Waddah's death I began to treat Adnan like Waddah. I sheltered him from regime raids in the early days of the pro-democracy protests, and when Adnan helped spearhead the early armed resistance in Moadamiya, I worried about him constantly.

In August 2012, when the regime attacked the neighbouring town of Daraya and killed over 1,200 people in just a hundred hours, many young men from Moadamiya, Damascus and southern Syria streamed into the town in an unsuccessful effort to resist the assault. Adnan was one of them, killed by a sniper's bullet like so many other rebels during that battle. The news of Adnan's death hit me like a bolt of lightning; I grieved his passing almost as much as I had mourned the loss of my brother. And when that bullet from a Hezbollah sniper hurled me to the ground over a year later, I felt certain that I was about to suffer the same fate as Adnan.

I missed all of my friends, yet I also envied them because they had left this world martyrs. In Islam it is believed that if you die a *shaheed* – martyr – all your sins will be forgiven, and you will be admitted to the highest levels of paradise. They had died young, strong and brave, and most importantly they had died free, which was exactly how I wanted to go. One of my greatest fears was to be taken prisoner by the regime and to die in some rotten cell. I was determined to avoid such a fate, even if it meant that I died a little earlier.

As the situation steadily worsened, I began to feel as though I was stuck in a dream world. I spent countless hours on Skype, Facebook, satellite phone and any other means of communication I could get hold of, recounting the horrors we were experiencing and pleading for help. But I could no longer believe that the harsh realities I was describing were true. I could not believe that, in the year 2013, I was pleading endlessly with the world to end this living hell without seeing any results. At some point my meagre diet of olives, coffee and the world's endless stream of empty promises would no longer sustain me.

I stopped sleeping. I refused to take sleeping pills, but when I did sleep, I wanted to stay asleep for ever, until my nightmare came to an end. When I woke up, I did not accept that I was truly awake. I had to splash water on my face several times to convince myself that I was experiencing real life, and even then I had doubts. I knew that I had to take drastic action. If I continued like this, it was only a matter of time before I killed myself in one way or another.

I decided that I needed my own totem, something to keep me grounded. I went to Abu Adnan, the architecture student turned bomb maker, and asked him for a weapon unique in Moadamiya. He gave me a prototype of a hand grenade that he had made only once, and I painted it bright green and yellow to ensure that there was no other grenade like it. When the paint dried, I stuck the grenade in my pocket and carried it with me at all times. Whenever I doubted that what I was living was real, I stood alone somewhere and held the grenade in my left hand, contemplating what would happen if I detonated it.

One day at around noon I was walking around Moadamiya taking pictures for *Channel 4 News* in Britain when a MiG warplane suddenly appeared. It swooped down, dropped its payload just metres away from me and whooshed away in a second. I saw the red fireball as the bomb exploded, and I was hurled back through the air. An excruciating pain shot through my back as I slammed into a wall. I noticed that there was a warm, red substance all over my body. There had been a little girl playing near me, right where the bomb had hit only seconds before. Now she was gone.

I scrabbled at my torso and face with my hands in a vain effort to remove all the blood from my body, and then took off through the streets of Moadamiya at top speed, as if possessed, in a desperate search for water to wash myself. When I could find no water, I simply stopped short and ripped my clothes off in the middle of the street where I stood.

That was when the grenade fell out of my pocket.

I grabbed it.

Looked for my lighter.

Found it.

Flicked on the lighter.

Stared at the flame and the fuse on the grenade.

For several fateful minutes I thought over and over about putting the flame to the fuse. I was in a state of total bewilderment. Only when I heard people calling my name did I rejoin the world and tuck the grenade back into my pocket. In all my time under siege in Moadamiya I never came closer to lighting my grenade; that is how desperate I was. But something – the will to live, I suppose – stopped me. But after I had put the grenade away, a new madness surged through my veins. I wanted revenge.

I ran home, grabbed my M4 and battle vest, and charged like a bull towards the front line. Every bird in the sky, every rock on the ground, every object in my entire world was screaming at me to take revenge for that little girl. I rushed into a building and clambered up the stairwell until I reached a perfect sniping height. Impatiently I adjusted my rifle sights, then scanned the Officers' Residence in search of a target. I wanted to kill as many soldiers as possible before they discovered my position. When they did, I would keep shooting as the bullets flew past me until one found its mark, and I fell to the ground and was reunited with all of my dear martyred friends.

The first person I saw was an officer sitting with his wife and son. The man and woman were sipping coffee and chatting, while the boy was in his own little world, savouring every little bite of the chocolate bar in his hand. I hadn't had chocolate for at least a year. I aimed the rifle at the father's head, took a long, deep breath and let the memories of the hundreds of people I had seen murdered by Assad's forces flash through my mind. I recalled the awful scent of rotted flesh, the searing burn of sarin in my lungs and the living death of starvation that this officer had helped to cause. When I pulled the trigger, I would begin to avenge all that.

I decided to look at each of their faces before taking the shot. The son seemed very innocent, with his big glasses and his T-shirt with some cartoon figure on it. He had stopped eating his chocolate and was now staring longingly at some other kids playing in the street. Surely he was dying to join them; I am not sure why his parents kept him from doing so. Perhaps they just really loved him and wanted to be sure that he was safe from harm. He was just a child. I felt sorry for the kid. He had two bastards for parents.

The mother was most likely a teacher, since she was holding what looked like school papers and had a pen in her hand. I wondered how she saw her husband off to work each day: 'Bye, sweetie! Have a good day! Kill all the terrorists you can, and don't forget to pick up the groceries on your way back!' *I'm sure she knows exactly what's happening in Syria: the revolution, the arrests, the bombardments and all the massacres that killers like her husband have perpetrated.*

I trained my scope back on the officer's head to take the shot, but at that moment I stopped seeing him as a soldier, even though he was wearing his uniform. I saw him as a father and husband. He could not keep his eyes or his smile off his son, and he never stopped teasing his beloved wife as she tried to mark her papers. I could not believe that they looked so much like a warm, happy family. They were enjoying their daily lives as if nothing was wrong with the world, as if neither I nor my friends were languishing in a living hell that they had created just one sniper shot away.

I flinched as I heard Assad's artillery slam shells into the town behind me, and they did not even blink.

Suddenly the boy threw his chocolate on the ground, burst into tears and pointed animatedly at the kids on the street. The father stood and picked his son up, holding and playing with him until he started to laugh again, then put him down and said a few words that made him jump for joy and run inside.

I lowered my rifle.

I have often replayed that moment in my head, and to this day I do not know if I made the right decision. I would be lying if I denied that I desperately wanted to shoot that officer, but I could not stop thinking about his son. If the regime survives, he will most likely grow up to be like his father. That little boy has no idea how much he is being deceived. I'm sure the officer's son has asked him many times about the awful sound of shells slamming into Moadamiya. No doubt the child wonders what has happened to all his friends who suddenly stopped coming to school in the early days of the revolution. I'm sure he has asked his father a million questions, just as I once asked my own baba a million questions. I'm certain that, unlike my baba, this officer did not tell his son the truth.

Humans are evil by nature. Allah said it, Freud based his theories on it, and the reality is clear: we all have a savage primal instinct, a drive to pursue our own basic urges regardless of right and wrong. But Allah also gave us the capacity to be noble, to control our basic instincts through legal codes, and to determine the most decent way to get what we want. Education goes a long way towards determining whether savagery or nobility wins out.

I used to wonder why all my Alawite and Shiite friends joined the army or security forces, while all my Sunni friends pursued careers in business. It once puzzled me that the Alawites and Shiites obtained so many leadership positions, even though 75 per cent of the Syrian population is Sunni. And why did the Alawites always live on hilltops, in the mountains and at the entrances to each city and town? Why did they never live in downtown areas, except in the Alawite heartland of Latakia and in the capital, Damascus?

If you want to win any battle, you have to control the resources and the terrain. Decades before the revolution began, the Alawites in Syria had already taken control of all the power: the guns, the money, the communications networks, the supply routes and the elevated areas. Government propaganda told us that these measures were necessary to fight Israel, but in truth the Syrian people were always the Assad family's main target and the Alawites their willing tools. They might have been reluctant, they might have had their reservations and regrets, but at the end of the day most Alawites fell in line and played their parts in the Assad family's murderous scheme.

When Assad's supporters suppressed protests early in the revolution, they chanted, 'Assad or we burn the country!' while his Alawite paramilitaries later fulfilled this vow by destroying Syrian towns and villages. As they did so, they cried, 'Syria is Assad's!' to let us all know that Syria belonged not to its citizens but to one family. While the *Shabiha* were brutal and savage, they were not crazy. Their parents had made up their minds to kill us years before they were even born.

Hafez al-Assad set the plan in motion when he seized power in the 1970s. He brainwashed thousands, perhaps millions of Syrians to hate all of his opponents and to annihilate anyone who dared question his rule. He then monopolized every means of power to ensure that the victims of his trained killers would never have the means to resist. When Hafez al-Assad passed away, he bequeathed this machinery of death to his son. All Bashar had to do was give the order, and armies of vicious merce-naries would rush to obey.

Perhaps it was out of frustration that we, the youth of Syria, had dared to hope and dream of a better future. Our parents had betrayed us by sleepwalking through their whole lives. They should have known after the Hama massacre of 1982 that the Assad family was too brutal to be allowed to hold power for another generation. They should have screamed their lungs out, fought tooth and nail, and struggled with all of their force after seeing what brutality the Assad regime was capable of. Instead, they kept silent as Hafez al-Assad set in motion a murderous plan to annihilate his future opponents. We, the youth of Syria, turned out to be those future opponents – and because our parents' generation kept silent, we paid a price in blood.

Hunger diaries
October–December 2013

The war was edging into a third winter. The siege of Moadamiya had taken its toll – almost 80 per cent of the town was destroyed: infrastructure, roads, schools, hospitals and mosques. More than 800 people had been killed, over 3,000 injured and thousands detained in Assad's prisons.

Starvation had sucked the life and hope out of everyone in the town, including me. But I couldn't just give up. I racked my brain for a way to bring attention to what was happening to us – and that's when I came up with the idea of a hunger strike. I might as well declare one; I was going to die from hunger anyway, so why not make it count? The world would be forced to confront our suffering. Some activists in the United States and Canada – Bayan Khatib and Mohja Kahf – helped me to get this idea off the ground. I had met them on Facebook as they were all following the revolution and had Syrian roots. Two American peace activists, Terry and Andy Burke were also involved in my hunger strike from its beginning. They advised me on the content of my blog and how to publicize the hunger strike through Skype group calls, and suggested calling for sympathy hunger strikes around the world in solidarity with Syria's starving people. The solidarity hunger strikers would experience, at least for a day, what every Moadamiya resident went through on an ongoing basis. On the activists' advice, I kept a public diary of my experiences during the hunger strike, throughout which I drank water and ate olives every few days. This is what happened.

Hunger strike day 1: Beginnings
Posted 26 November 2013
Today the hunger strike begins.

I am a 28-year-old Palestinian Syrian who serves the civilian local council of Moadamiya, Syria, protecting my family by using the pseudonym Qusai Zakarya.

Moadamiya, where I grew up and live, has been under siege for over 365 days. There are still 8,000 civilians living here, and our food supplies have run out. As a citizen journalist, I am now documenting my townspeople dying of hunger. Seven children and four women have already died of malnutrition.

Numerous humanitarian organizations have pleaded to no avail with the Assad regime to break the savage siege against civilians in cities throughout Syria, including Daraya, Yarmouk Camp, eastern Gouta and Homs. Assad continues to use food and medicine as weapons of war.

I declare a hunger strike beginning on Tuesday, November 26, until the siege against the townsfolk of Moadamiya is lifted.

I call on people of conscience everywhere to pressure their governments to act to break Assad's siege and let humanitarian agencies bring food and medicine into besieged areas.

Your support is my only weapon.

Hunger strike day 2: Remembering Rana
Posted 27 November 2013
I hold on . . .

It's the second day of my hunger strike. The pain of hunger is with me all day but I've got used to hunger. Food supplies ran out about four months ago, after being under siege for over a year, and there's been very little to eat ever since. I wake up to hunger. I sleep with hunger. Hunger is with me all day long. The hunger strike only intensifies the pain and adds exhaustion to the mix.

I talked to many journalists today. I'm so glad the story is getting out there. I hope that I will be able to make a difference. After a dozen calls with bad Internet connection and my stomach rumbling in constant reminder of my mission, I feel depleted.

There are moments when I feel weak. During those times I remember the children I watched starve to death. I remember little Rana . . . and I hold on.

Hunger strike day 3: Lost and distraught
Posted 28 November 2013
Today I lost consciousness. I've survived many bombings but the last one that fell close to our house three weeks ago sent me flying against the wall. I thought I was OK but then I started to have severe back pain. Yesterday the pain spread from my back down to my left leg. The pain is so bad that it overpowers the hunger.

I went to the doctor in our town. He said there's nothing he can do to help me without the medical equipment

he needs. Someone gave me four pills. Painkillers, I think.
I took them. I got dizzy and blacked out, probably because
I took the pills on an empty stomach. I woke up a couple
of hours later feeling lost and distraught. I can't remember
anything. I want to keep track of which media I spoke to
but I can't remember.

Human Rights Watch called me today. That I remember. I hope they will be able to help.

My head hurts. The world is spinning. I am lying on
the floor and I cannot get up. I have asked my friend to
write this post for me today.

Hunger strike day 4: The regime tries to make a deal
Posted 29 November 2013
Instead of allowing food into besieged areas, the regime
pressures Syrians to evacuate or face starvation, adding to
the displacement crisis.

Today was another exhausting day. Problems keep
piling up. This time the regime sent a committee of five
people originally from our town but now living outside it
to present a deal to us.

Starving a population is illegal. Food should have no
preconditions. The regime proposes a conditional ceasefire
with the FSA living in our town, but made ridiculous and illegal preconditions! They want us to raise the regime flag inside
Moadamiya and they also want all those who are not originally from Moadamiya to leave the town. That means me too,
because I'm originally Palestinian. Even though I grew up in
this town, they don't count me as a real citizen of Moadamiya.

Their demands are stupid and meant to strip us of our
dignity and displace us. Displaced Syrians suffer unspeakable agonies. I don't want to become yet another displaced
Syrian – adding to my displaced history as a Palestinian.

In return for these ridiculous and racist demands, they agree to consider – only consider – allowing some food back into the town. They may allow just a little bit of food per day, maybe enough for one meal for each person. Basically, they want to keep control of food. Even if they agree to let some food in, they will do it in a way where they are still in control and can cut it off once again whenever they want.

The townspeople have not come to a decision. The regime made the offer in such a way as to cause problems between the people inside. There is heated debate among the people. Hunger makes people not think straight any more. I am afraid that the Council will decide to hand the regime our town on a silver platter. Regime forces have been trying to get into the town for months now, and we've been trying to keep them out. We know if they come in it means all of us will be slaughtered with knives . . . as this was the fate of several other towns in Syria once the regime was able to break in.

This whole negotiation is simply to add more pressure on the people to kneel to Assad's will. They know how badly we are in need of food and medicine and they are manipulating our desperation, hoping we will give up on our demand for freedom.

In the midst of this chaos I hold on to my conviction in protesting against this oppression through my hunger strike.

After a long and tiring day, I lie on my mattress, aware that my weakened body is trapped under siege in Moadamiya, but a strange feeling overcomes me, a feeling that my spirit is free, free to visit all the places I love in Syria, to walk the streets where I used to work and where my friends and I hung out, free to go to Homs, where I went for university. This strange feeling leaves me happy.

My body is depleted and exhausted but my spirit is free and happy.

Hunger strike day 5: Her name is Sara . . .
Posted 30 November 2013
Today my back pain was severe again. I decided to go to the field hospital and see if they could give me anything to help with the pain. When I walked into the hospital, I heard a girl crying and screaming. I ran to where the noise was coming from and found a little girl in the emergency room. The minute I saw her, I forgot my own pain.

The girl's name is Sara. She's five years old. The doctors were changing the bandages on her burned face. She was burned by one of Assad's bombs. Two weeks ago she was asleep in her home when a bomb fell on her house. I grabbed a camera and filmed Sara. I wanted to show the world what Assad was doing to the children of Syria. After seeing Sara, I walked back home in a daze. There were bombardments all around but I didn't seem to care.

I've been meaning to make a video to share on my blog . . . seeing Sara gave me the energy I needed to get up and get it done. I asked my friend Anas to help me. He followed me around so we could describe the destruction of our town. Damn Assad.

I can't get Sara's burned face or her screams out of my head. When will the world ever wake up?

Hunger strike day 6: Fantasies and death threats
Posted 1 December 2013
'Patience and endurance.'

We will endure. We will overcome.

Today I fantasized about abandoning my hunger strike and slaughtering a donkey like some men here in Moadamiya did a few days ago, feeding as many women and children as possible with it. A full meal and a cigarette, how good that would feel! I'm happy that my hunger strike touched so many people around the world, that it raised awareness about Assad's use of food as a tool of war, and so I won't let these thoughts go further than fantasies and words. God has blessed me, and my friends, with endurance we never thought possible before the revolution.

Our town was chaos today. The townspeople were in upheaval about regime negotiations and the potential ceasefire. Even while five men sent by the regime sat among us, selling the regime's story, the regime was shelling our town. Yes, even as they tried to convince us to take their dirty deal, illegally placing conditions on food reaching civilians, the regime once again attacked our town using ruthless military force. Only in the twisted mind of the regime could this behaviour make sense.

Our biggest fear remains that the regime will be able to get in . . . as this means certain death for the activists in Moadamiya. They will slaughter us with knives like they did to many innocent civilians before us. I often think about the many ways I can avoid this fate.

After much thought, I decided to make a video detailing something I had refused to speak about before, which is that I've been receiving death threats from people inside and outside Moadamiya. I don't want to write in detail about it here, as it may further endanger my life, but I feel better knowing that I have sent this video to my friends here and abroad, so that if something does happen to me, they will know the circumstances and understand who is responsible.

While my body aches with hunger and pain and my mind swirls with worries of regime invasion and death threats, inside I feel at peace. I am ready to accept whatever God wills for me.

Hunger strike day 7: Overshadowing pain
Posted 2 December 2013
My slipped disc caused me unbearable pain today. I wanted to scream, hit my head against a wall, anything to ease the pain. The pain travelled to my left leg and I cannot move it. There's so much going on in the town, but the pain overshadowed the commotion around me.

If I wasn't in so much pain I might worry about having to leave town in a few days if the townspeople are forced to give in to the regime's illegal conditions for the cease-fire. It seems this might happen soon. Among their arbitrary conditions, before they implement the ceasefire, they want everyone who isn't originally from Moadamiya out. That's right, this regime wants to throw me out of the town I grew up in and love, because I'm of Palestinian origin.

I don't know where I'll go if that happens. I can't think that far ahead right now. I'm sorry I can't write much today. Hopefully tomorrow the pain will subside and I can explain more about what's happening here.

Hunger strike day 8: What dreams may come
Posted 3 December 2013
I spent most of the day in bed, but I had sweet memories to keep me company. Last night, after taking a strong painkiller, I slept for a long time and had a strange yet

wonderful dream. In my dream I walked around our town, stopped by the corner shop, the one my neighbour owns, and it was stocked full of food. Sweets mostly. Biscuits and chocolates of every sort! I grabbed a pack of cookies off the shelf, ripped it open and gobbled down as many as I could. I devoured one cookie after another, and the shop owner stared at me with a 'What on earth are you doing?' expression on his face. But I didn't care. The pleasure of feeling those cookies fill my stomach was so good.

Next thing I know, I was at the border of Moadamiya and Daraya at my favourite fast-food restaurant, where my friends and I had eaten hundreds of meals. I walked in and told the owner to make me one of every sandwich on the menu: burger, chicken kebab and crispy. Crispy was my favourite sandwich. It was made with crispy fried chicken breast. And some fries too, I told the guy, and of course lots and lots of soda.

Next, I was at my friends' and my favourite pastry shop. My best friend showed up. He hadn't seen me in a long time so he wanted to greet me with the Syrian customary kiss on each cheek, but I was like, 'Hey, man, get me some *hareesa* with *semna* (buttery ghee) and *'ishta* (clotted cream). We can greet each other later!! There's *hareesa* in there, and I want it.'

I slept for a long time last night, longer than my body usually allows me to sleep, maybe because of the painkillers or maybe because I was getting to eat all my favourite foods, and that's not the sort of dream you want to wake up from.

As I spent the day in bed, I thought about how before the siege, and before the revolution, food was the centre of our lives. All my friends and I ever did was hang out at our favourite food places and indulge in Syria's amazing

delicacies. Oh, how things have changed. God willing,
once the regime falls, Syria will be back and better than
ever.

Hunger strike day 9: Crossroads
Posted 4 December 2013
I have a really bad feeling about where these negotiations
are heading. The regime's arbitrary conditions are designed
to shatter our dignity and give the regime a propaganda
victory. This revolution started for freedom and dignity.
Some of the local council members want to give up our
dignity and for what? The regime won't even break off the
siege. They will simply allow tiny rations of food in every
day – if they even live up to that. Not one of us trusts the
regime, no matter what else we disagree on.

There are corrupt people among the negotiators
on both sides. They are pushing hard for the ceasefire
despite humiliating regime preconditions, such as the
racist demand that everyone who isn't a 'pure' original
Moadamiyan be expelled, and that the town fly the regime
flag. The fact that the regime is pushing so hard for this
shows it is under pressure. The regime badly needs an
open route for its troops through Moadamiya. We should
hold on until we get what we deserve: to lift the siege.
Food is a basic human right. I am so frustrated with those
townspeople who are willing to sell our town short.

I've spoken up against this bad deal and now I've been
threatened with death if I don't shut up and stop trying
to influence the discussion. Some of my close friends have
been threatened too, if they don't let the negotiators get
their way. These are the tactics some people have learned
from a lifetime living under this regime.

Only the day will tell what will unfold.

Hunger strike day 10: Something smells rotten here in Moadamiya
Posted 5 December 2013

Food cooked by the 4th Division of Assad's army, world famous for their skill in carving human limbs: would you eat it?

It's not a joke. Besides expelling me from town for having Palestinian origins, the regime is actually saying in its underhanded negotiations here in my hometown that 'food must be cooked by the 4th Division'. That is the regime's precondition for anything people in the town of Moadamiya eat. Our local council is carefully studying it . . .

You know when you have this uneasy feeling that the waiter might have spat in your food? That, multiplied by a capacity for evil beyond the imagination of most people reading this blog, is making a lot of stomachs in Moadamiya more nauseous than usual right now.

Palestinians under occupation [by the Israelis] are being denied access to water. Syrians – and this Palestinian Syrian – are being denied access to wholesome food. I want to hear the world's outrage.

Food justice is a basic human right. Without preconditions. Food – not poison.

What else could they be up to besides poisoning us? The answer is: degradation.

They're not lifting the siege and letting humanitarian convoys bring bags of rice and flour, oh no. The very capable women of Moadamiya would love to get their hands on some staples to cook. No. The regime wants to dole it out bite by bite, like prison rations, to control us on a daily basis.

You know what? This regime takes the prize for trickery. I'm not sure if most people outside Syria understand how amazingly deceitful this regime is with its media spin. I mean who would have thought you could take a straightforward demand, 'Food now,' and twist it by saying, 'You will take only these scrapings of food, directly from our bloodstained hands that have been murdering you, and you will do it now, on our degrading terms.' Then they will boast in front of the world that they're giving us food and try to destroy the momentum we are gaining for serious international humanitarian aid to more than one and a half million starving people in Syria's besieged cities.

When you think about it, actually, starvation has been used for decades by the regime to keep us on a leash, like a dog led to its dish to keep it submissive. What else does it mean to have a country where most people cannot earn enough to put food on their tables from month to month, where the ruling family and its buddies skim off every working person's life by extortion and bribery? Where people driven by the need to eat a bit of bread are willing to accept humiliation, as if it was normal for humans to live without freedom, without dignity, without justice?

We demand that international chefs come in to watch Maher and his 4th Division cook our food.

Hunger strike day 11: The sweet sound of shelling
Posted 6 December 2013
I wake up to the familiar sound of shelling coming from the regime's 4th Division in their mountain positions. Strangely, it feels good this time to wake up to the noise of Assad raining shells on us. Maybe because it helps the townspeople in Moadamiya to remember that we cannot trust the Assad regime. One day they send negotiators. The next day they shell us. Again.

Oh, and the regime just added another precondition for food: Qusai Zakarya (that's me . . .) has to be handed over. They like media people. Before the children can eat, the regime also demands certain local council leaders and FSA commanders be delivered into their loving hands.

My bad back is killing me, and I am starting to lose control of my left leg, so I go again today to the field hospital to have the doctors check me. Not minding the heavy shelling, I start walking through Moadamiya's streets. My hometown is covered with dirt and mud, because it has been raining all night, and when the bombs explode in the ground mud covers lots of the buildings in Moadamiya. What a strange yet beautiful scene . . .

At the hospital I expect to find lots of wounded civilians. But I guess since Christmas is coming, we had an early Christmas miracle – no one so far has been struck by a shell. But rest in peace, Mahmoud Hamdan Abo Obeid, a town elder who died of malnutrition today.

A lot of people are at the field hospital. They are hiding there from the heavy shelling because the hospital is in a basement. All of them are saying, 'To hell with negotiating a truce; the Assad regime will never change and we can never trust them.'

My townsfolk's high spirits make me forget my pain and smile.

Hunger strike, day 12: Finding strength in shattered minarets
Posted 7 December 2013
It was the rain of shells. The shelling yesterday brought down the minaret of the Rawda Mosque, where we all used to gather before going into the street to shout, 'Freedom!' and, 'The people want the fall of the regime!'

Seeing that minaret cut down on the ground was like a wound for all of us. Have you ever seen a landmark of your land crushed by the bombs of an enemy?

The shelling did not only bring down the minaret. The shelling brought down the regime's negotiations for a ceasefire. It changed something inside my town, my Moadamiya. Seeing that minaret down yesterday made us all remember the early days of peaceful protests and the friends we have lost to regime bullets since those days.

My buddy and near neighbour was one of them, a young man in his prime. We called him Abu al-Khayr, and he was killed about a year ago. Then there was a town elder everyone used to call 'the mufti'. His name was Said Douba; he was killed by the regime. There are others, so many to mourn. So many recent widows, so many recent orphans. So much grief.

Suddenly the idea of handing over fifty of our own townspeople into the arms of the regime started to taste sour to most of the people in Moadamiya. It tasted like betrayal. Those Council members among us who still argued today for meeting all the regime's demands and preconditions were talking in the wind. Because even for starving people, betrayal can make you more nauseous than hunger.

Hunger strike day 13: Not just a movie . . .
Posted 8 December 2013
They're burning the earth today. Fierce shelling by the regime forces surrounding Moadamiya – ground-to-ground rockets, MiGs. It felt like 500 shells exploded on this town today. Four of them barely missed me.

Five of my townspeople were wounded in today's bombing. They had to be dragged inside. Two of them were little kids – a girl and a boy. Unlike the Helm's Deep battle in *Lord of the Rings*, which I've seen a million times, there are no caves where the children and women can hide. They're doing their best in basements. In the movie the enemy army got blinded for a minute by the rising sun, right when reinforcements ride on their horses to save all the people. We need the sun to help us, a bunch of charging horses – anything.

So far, the FSA brigades at the edges of town are holding the 'Orcs' back. The talk is that the regime is going to try again to storm the town tomorrow, big time.

Hunger strike day 14: Hell unleashed
Posted 9 December 2013
It just keeps raining on Moadamiya.

Ten tanks are reportedly headed this way from the regime's military airbase at Mezze right now. So tomorrow looks to be another red hellish day of regime assault on my hometown. I'm going to the front with my camera, and to be honest, if I'm needed, I'll help the defence. I'm not going to abandon my friends and not defend my town.

The hungry are still hungry. That's all for now. I'm exhausted and need to get some rest.

Hunger strike day 15: The Syrian revolution huddle – for the win! Posted 10 December 2013
Cold down to my bones. Three pairs of socks, layers of clothes later – still cold in my dark basement. Back pain has travelled down into my leg, but I walk to the home of a friend with a fireplace – must get warm.

A fireplace is a treasure in Moadamiya. Gathering wood is really risky, because the woods of Moadamiya are right under the 4th Division's scopes. So people burn anything instead – plastic bottles, bags. Heat is worth the fumes. Besides, after surviving sarin gas, what's a little bit of fumes, right?

Family and friends huddle around the fire, about a dozen of us, kids and adults, men and women. (And if the extremist armed Islamists in other parts of Syria don't like that, they can kiss my arse. Moadamiya hasn't had to deal with them up close, so far – and I think their presence is exaggerated in the media. A lot of guys look Islamist but aren't. Long beards are just easier than shaving.)

My stomach is empty, the coffee is mostly water, but my spirit is full of blessings. We have so many victories to count. We have won knowledge of how brave Syrians are, a whole generation of us. We have won ourselves.

Never mind the regime tanks, and the shelling (twice today). Shelling is boring. Barça's chances, that's the buzz around the fire. Real Madrid sucks! Go, Barça! The next game is super important. Will players keep the faith?

Hunger strike day 16: The scream
Posted 11 December 2013
I can't feel my toes. They're frozen. God damn it to hell. Yes, the fire of hell would be very useful right now for the children of Syria freezing to death in the besieged towns and the refugee camps this winter.

The heat of hell could ease some of the pain I am feeling right now in both of my freezing legs, so I can get out of my basement and go walking in the streets of Moadamiya and scream out loud, Fuck you, Bashar, and fuck each and every person standing behind you, and fuck all the corrupt ones among the rebels and FSA leaders whose idiocy let Bashar get us to this point.

God. I want to punch the sky and fight with the wind to stop it from freezing a starved people. Stop it! Stop adding to the suffering of homeless refugees.

God forgive me, and please give us your mercy and strength to fight the cold. God damn the cold.

People in my town are trying to gather anything they can find from the rubble of the destroyed houses, wood, plastic, anything blowing in the wind.

Oh my darling Syria, what have they done to you?

Killed, raped, bombed, displaced, gassed, starved and now frozen, your sons and daughters, just because they didn't want to see you a free lady choosing your own lover.

Hush, hush now, don't cry or you are going to make me start crying too, Syria. It's a dark freezing night. Cover yourself well and sleep on your wounds another night and have a sweet dream about your knight in shining armour coming on a fast horse, and let me have my own sweet dream about the hot fire of hell.

Hunger strike day 18: Nights of sorrow
Posted 13 December 2013

Northern nights of sorrow
Go on remember me, remember me
My beloved asks about me
Northern nights of sorrow
Oh, my love, I am a bird in the field
My family promised me to the sun and the street
Oh, my love.

It's a song by Fairouz. I've been listening to it over and over since since yesterday. It makes me feel high, in a strange way. Maybe because the lyrics echo what's going on in my head? The sad winter taking what's left of our smiles, the emptiness I feel when I walk the destroyed streets of our town, my family and my mum, who I haven't seen in over a year and a half, and my girlfriend, my love, who stopped talking to me a few months ago because she fears that she'll call asking about me one day and find that I'm dead due to shelling, starvation or any of the other ways Assad is killing us.

A blanket of beautiful white snow has covered Moadamiya, which has disrupted my Internet connection. I normally love snow, but these days its beauty can harbour deadliness. How can I be so selfish, spending time thinking about my shadows of happiness while more than twenty-five people, including women and children, froze to death yesterday in our besieged towns, in the refugee camps and in Assad's prisons? I heard that over a dozen prisoners froze to death in Aleppo's central prison. I know well how they make you sit in those tiny cold cells without any clothes, or if you're lucky, in your underwear. In a winter such as this one, they must have known that those bodies would not survive.

A Syria where human life and dignity are respected, that's what we're fighting for, and I know that one day it will be ours.

But tonight is another night of sorrow. Syrian nights of sorrow.

Hunger strike day 20: Stop blaming Alexa!
Posted 15 December 2013
Wasn't able to write yesterday because I was so mad at the entire world. I was freezing in body, burning in heart.

I walked around Moadamiya while the snow was falling, and I saw my town covered with white death. The thick snow killed the simple vegetables that some families tried to plant to feed themselves.

Many children were taken to our field hospital to get treated for very bad colds, and there was nothing the doctors could do except give them painkillers because we are very short of medicine.

Doctors are also treating a lot of Moadamiya civilians for stomach pains and worms and other digestive problems related to eating things that may not be fit for eating. Leaves of random trees, domestic animals . . . who knows what has gone into their guts these four months.

Left the field hospital angry as a bull. Went back home forgetting all about my freezing starved body and killing bad back pain. Signed into Facebook and Skype to do some work, but all I saw was more Syrian kids frozen to death, more shit about Geneva 2, the expansion of the Islamic extremists in the FSA, more crap about a new truce the regime is planning to offer us, and of course more dumbheads who are willing to fall for this trick again.

Damn it. I felt my heart pumping fire instead of blood through my body.

I felt that, in a way, all the world has the icy blood of the freezing children of Syria on its hands, starting with Bashar the damn Assad and his allies, the hypocrites of the Western governments who care about getting rid of Assad's chemicals but don't care about the damage his other weapons are doing, the greedy politicians of the Syrian opposition, and let's not forget corrupt FSA leaders, and even my small attempts to make a difference.

One way or another, we all have the iced blood of the freezing children of Syria on our hands, so please stop blaming Storm Alexa!

Hunger strike day 23: Even the trees are their enemies
Posted 18 December 2013

The trees help us. The olive orchards and lemon trees of Moadamiya are more than just a livelihood. They are friends and allies. More – they are the living legacy of my townsfolk. We love each tree. We know them from childhood, each knot. They put their arms around us. They shade our first love, our family picnics. Some are 400 years old.

Think about that. What have these trees seen? What tyrants come and go while they stay, patient and wise? While they draw water from deep in the ground and put out their green and yellow fruit with generosity, year after year.

So of course, of course, the Assad regime has been deliberately targeting our beautiful olive groves, on the west and south-west sides of Moadamiya, with its shelling, from the start and even more intensely nowadays.

Assad's forces want to destroy our livelihood.

They want to destroy a food source for the townspeople.

They are killing our friends, the trees we love.

How can I describe to you the emotions we in Moadamiya feel when we see these trees killed? Bombed and shelled and broken . . . My parents suffered the loss of their olive trees in a Palestinian village in 1948. Today, when an olive tree falls from Zionist violence in Palestine, the whole activist world mourns. Whole groves of trees are shelled in Syria, and no one hears the sound they make.

No one hears the branches crack and break but us. No one sees the roots shockingly torn above the exploded ground but us.

Hear the trees. If you will not hear the human screams in Syria, hear the ancient screams of the trees.

Hunger strike day 27: General Hummel's trousers
Posted 22 December 2013

Today the weather was a little warmer than usual, so I decided to wash my trousers. I know this sounds like a mundane event, but it's actually quite complicated.

We don't have heating at home. Because of the siege we haven't had electricity or gas in over a year. So I had to wait for warm weather to wash my trousers. I've only got this one pair, so when I wash them, I wear my pyjamas, but pyjamas alone aren't much protection against the cold.

When I turned on the tap and ran my fingers through the freezing water, I changed my mind. It's been a couple of weeks since I washed them last and they're caked with dirt and mud. But with the water that cold, I just couldn't imagine hand-washing clothes, or anything else for that matter.

I've been through a lot with these trousers. I've been wearing them for many months now. Every other pair of trousers I owned have been destroyed in bombings or stolen.

It's no coincidence that these are my last pair of trousers. I'm wearing them somewhat reluctantly, as they belong to my eldest brother, who's fled the country now, and I didn't want to ruin them for him.

My brother used to be thinner than me, and his trousers would have never fit me before. Now that I've lost so much weight, they fit just about right.

I sewed these trousers about four times and stitched up tiny tears dozens of times. Mum taught me how to sew a long time ago. With so many kids in the house, we all had to pitch in to help her. I learned to cook, wash dishes and sew.

These trousers have quite a history, even long before they became my one and only pair. *The Rock* is one of my brother's and my favourite movies ever. We watched it about 200 times, and my brother became completely obsessed with getting a pair of trousers just like General Hummel's (General Hummel is played by the actor Ed Harris in the movie). So he searched far and wide until finally, in Lebanon, he found a fabric that seemed just right. He brought it home and had a seamstress make him a pair of trousers just like General Hummel's.

I don't know how many more stitch jobs my General Hummel trousers can take, or how I will manage if anything happens to them. I know that I'm better off than some of the Syrian refugees who fled their homes with nothing but the clothes on their backs. Or those who fled in the summer and must survive the harsh winter with only their flimsy summer clothes.

Hunger strike day 29: Starving on Christmas
Posted 24 December 2013
'Starving on Christmas' was the name of the report I wanted to shoot for the US news network NBC in the besieged city of Daraya, which is separated from our beloved Moadamiya by a huge regime checkpoint manned by Assad mercenaries.

I went there yesterday afternoon to shoot the churches destroyed by the Assad shelling and bombardment and to try to talk to some Christian families about how they will spend this Christmas under siege, with empty stomachs and frozen bodies, no trees to decorate and no presents to give to their poor kids.

I got shot on my way there – just a graze, nothing worth mentioning – and could not get the footage, so I am going to have to try again today, inshallah.

After being treated at the local hospital, I went home and managed to start a fire using some plastic and

wood which my friend had gathered from the rubble
of destroyed houses. I was humming George Michael's
song 'Last Christmas', which I can never keep out of my
head at Christmastime. For me, it rings bells of familiar
joy about spending Christmastime in the traditionally
Christian section of the old city of Damascus, Bab Touma
(Thomas Gate), where I used to go with my Christian
and Muslim friends to hang out late. Good times. Once
my friends challenged me to talk to this beautiful girl
and in return they'd buy me dinner, and I was broke like
the Great Depression, plus she was really cute. So I put
on a Santa hat and I approached where she was standing
with her friends and started to do my happy dance in
the middle of Bab Touma Square. Now I am an awful
dancer, but believe it or not she and her friends started
to dance with me, laughing. Within seconds a bunch of
guys and girls came along and joined us, but my friends
chickened out and stood there like ice men. I won the
dinner fair and square, and got the girl's number.

Ever since the exposure of Bashar's flirty email corre-
spondence with his female aide who called him her duckie,
we call him the Duck just for fun, and duck-heads has
become a nickname for his supporters. Some duck-heads,
such as the notorious Mother Agnes-Maryam, talk about
Assad's protection for Christians and other minorities. But
in Syria Christians and Muslims were living as brothers
and sisters hundreds of years before Assad, and he is not
the force protecting Syrians of any religion – our human
values are. And having an accountable government in a
future Syria, one that guarantees human rights equally
for all Syrians, will be the best protection for Christians,
not a dictator's whim. Lots of Christian Syrians are with
the revolution and want to see Assad behind bars as a war

criminal. One of them was a citizen-journalist like me,
trying to get footage of Assad's crimes out to the world; his
name was Basel Shehadeh, and he was killed by regime fire
while filming.

And guess what – like all the other folk, Christian
Syrians in besieged rebel towns are starving for Christmas.

Hunger strike day 30: We will never give up
Posted 25 December 2013
During another filthy truce offer from the regime to the
civilians of Moadamiya, Assad once again aimed at getting
us to give up on the revolution and return to being his
loyal servants, and he once again used food as a weapon in
attempt to make us kneel to his criminal demands.

Assad has been starving the besieged people of
Moadamiya for over a year, trying to make us desperate
enough to resort to any means to feed our families and
children. And so our local council has now agreed to raise
the regime flag over our town, as a first step in a bigger
deal. In return, the regime promises to deliver daily meals
to the town. This tactic will keep incoming food under
regime control. We will continue to be at their mercy for
every meal on a daily basis.

What we need is for the regime to break the siege and
allow the people Moadamiya open and free access to get
the food and medicine they need.

I cried like a five-year-old who had lost his mum
when I saw the regime flag over the Council building. I
remembered all of my friends who died for the sake of the
revolution and the others who continue to struggle in the
name of freedom and dignity. Dear God, what a feeling . . .

It's Christmas Day, and for the first time in my life I
truly wish that Santa was real so I could ask him for food

and medicine for all the besieged towns so we can be saved
from this humiliation and suffering. I don't know about
Santa, but I do know that I will keep going with my work,
supporting the struggle for freedom and human rights in
Syria. We will never ever give up.

*The following press release was prepared by my activist friends
in the US, Terry, Mohja and Bayan.*

QUSAI ENDS HIS HUNGER STRIKE

> Moadamiya, Syria, December 29, 2013: The Food Justice
> Baton Is Passed to the World by the Hunger Striker of
> Syria, and We Shall Uphold It

On November 26, Qusai Zakarya began a hunger strike
in a nonviolent action to demand that the Assad regime's
armed siege on the Syrian town of Moadamiya be lifted,
and that humanitarian agencies be allowed to bring food
and medicine to the dozens of besieged towns in Syria.

Due to health issues, Qusai decided to end his personal
hunger strike on December 29, his 33rd day. With this,
he passes the baton to the International Solidarity Hunger
Strike. 'Access to food for the populations of dozens of
Syrian towns that are still besieged and still starving,
remains critical,' Qusai says.

An International Solidarity Hunger Strike launched on
December 20, to support these goals. Philosophy luminar-
ies Jurgen Habermas, Seyla Benhabib, Slavoj Zizek, and
Hilary Putnam; Bahraini human rights activist Maryam
al-Khawaja; Syrian media activists Razan Ghazzawi and
Raed Fares, poets Marilyn Hacker and Martin Espada
and Syria's Khawla Dunia, joined the strike.

Our ranks expanded with prominent American public figures such as Bill Fletcher Jr., Noam Chomsky, Rabbi Lynn Gottlieb, Norman Finkelstein, Simon Critchley, and Congressman Keith Ellison. Solidarity hunger strikers include Andrei Codrescu of Romanian origin, as well as Omid Safi, Nader Hashemi, and Leila Zand, who are of Iranian origin, and novelists Robin Yassin-Kassab and Mohja Kahf, who are of Syrian origin. Syrian schoolteacher and protester Soad Nofal, Syrian writer Yassin al-Haj Saleh, and Syrian doctor Mazen Halabi, along with many other Syrians, joined. The response of Huwaids Arraf, Palestinian-American co-founder of the pro-Palestinian International Solidarity Movement, when she was invited to join the International Solidarity Hunger Strike for Syria was, 'Yes, without hesitation.'

The International Solidarity Hunger Strike is still growing and will continue until January 22, when the Geneva Conference on Syria convenes.

The team working on Qusai's Facebook page, including Bayan Khatib and Mohja Kahf, who are Syrian activists in North America, deeply appreciate Qusai's personal commitment to bringing international focus on the food blockade affecting one and a half million Syrians. 'Qusai is a valuable spokesperson for Moadamiya citizens, and for the Syrian revolution for freedom, human rights, and democracy,' says Terry Burke of the Minnesota-based Friends for a NonViolent World, who is also part of the team. She adds, 'We are grateful that Qusai ended the strike before suffering permanent damage to his health.'

Despite the recent submission of the local council of Moadamiya to humiliating conditions imposed by the Assad regime in exchange for regime promises of allowing food into the town, to date only a small amount of food has been allowed in by the regime: one truck with canned food inadequate even for one meal for the 8,000 civilians in Moadamiya. Local civilians, including Qusai, believe this is a cruel regime ploy to keep the town dependent on arbitrary regime conditions.

The Assad regime is still violating international law and still using food as a weapon of war not only in Moadamiya but in dozens of other Syrian towns that remain under starvation siege. International humanitarian agencies have not yet been allowed unfettered access to Moadamiya to distribute food and medicine, as required by the non-binding Statement of the United Nations' Security Council last September. We still need a binding UN resolution on this, and it must happen before the Geneva Conference convenes.

Qusai's act of civil resistance was bravely forged amid surrounding conditions of violence. His nonviolent action motivated many people around the world to join in solidarity with besieged and starving Syrian civilians. This solidarity is even more urgently needed as Qusai now passes the baton to all of us.

A dying town
31 December 2013–4 February 2014

I have never felt more lonely than I did the night after abandoning my hunger strike. It was New Year's Eve, a time when most of the world was celebrating, and when I myself would have once gathered with my friends to see in the new year. But there were no new year's parties in Moadamiya – only aimless and painful wanderings amid cold, silent ruins. My entire town was coloured dark shades of death and sadness.

New Year's Eve is always a sad day for me because it is the anniversary of my brother Waddah's sudden death. And on this particular day my feelings felt crushed into a sadness so deep it was almost physically unbearable as I thought of everything I had lost.

When the people of Moadamiya first demonstrated in the early days of the revolution, Assad's forces beat us, shot us and tortured to death those they arrested. We then got our hands on some light weapons to defend ourselves, and we survived eighteen months of air strikes, artillery bombardments, ground assaults and chemical attacks. But when the regime deployed starvation as a weapon against us, we eventually succumbed. After years of bombardment, Moadamiya residents somehow grew accustomed to the idea that they could die from a mortar bomb or a missile strike at any second, but we could not bear to watch as our friends and loved ones died slowly, in unbearable agony, over the course of many months.

No one had taught us how to protest, yet we demonstrated.

No one had taught us how to fight, yet we learned to defend our town.

No one had taught us that whoever controls the roads will ultimately win any fight, so we lost.

In the run-up to the ceasefire deal I no longer felt safe in my own town. I felt that even many of my oldest friends, blinded as they were by their starvation and misery, had come to view me as a stranger. They were turning on each other, and they turned on me too. I was asked why I cared about a ceasefire, told that I had nothing at stake, with my family gone and no children to worry about. I was called a traitor. I had long ago grown accustomed to death threats from the regime, but I could never have imagined that I would feel so insecure among my own people, who I had suffered so much with for three long years.

When the regime opened the northern checkpoints at the start of the ceasefire, many new faces entered Moadamiya. Hundreds of families, some returning, some entirely new and probably displaced from other more ravaged towns, but all with no money and no other place to go, streamed back into Moadamiya in a matter of days. The next time I went to check on my family's old apartment, I found a death threat addressed to me attached to the front door. Unknown callers rang my cellphone endlessly, leaving abusive messages. I remember words like burn, skin, torture, kill.

I feared that a regime agent or a desperate resident might try to kidnap me, so I had a friend upload a video of me with my grenade, making it clear to everyone that if I thought I was about to be taken I would blow myself and everyone around me to pieces.

When an international organization asked me to document Assad's new chlorine gas bombs in Daraya, I did not tell anyone I was going, not even friends I thought I could trust, because I was no longer sure I could trust anyone. I went alone. I spent several days talking to people who worked in the field hospitals there. I'd been told to collect blood samples, dirt from the impact sites and a fragment of a weapon, if I could find one. I got everything I could, including the serial number of a missile, but there was no way to get the evidence out, as security around the town was too tight. It was, ultimately, a pointless mission.

Despair, lack of sleep, insecurity and insufferable living conditions combined to make me feel that I was about to go insane. I now had to leave – I wanted out. For days and weeks I pondered routes that I could use to flee Moadamiya, accompanied by only a few trusted friends who were willing to fight their way out, but I could never quite bring myself to raise the idea with them. To make things worse, I got another mysterious call from an unknown caller – almost certainly on the regime side – who said they knew what I wanted to do, and there were many eyes on me. I would be captured if I tried to leave. Abu Omar, one of my closest friends throughout the siege, who shared my taste in music and food, told me that he had heard leaks from within the 4th Division of an officer discussing my plans for escape. I knew then that the regime was watching me too closely for me to able to sneak out of Moadamiya.

I knew I could not stay in Moadamiya any longer, but I knew that there was no way I could get out unnoticed. I was in an impossible position, which is the only way I can explain what I decided to do. I talked three of my friends, Abu Omar, Qutaiba and Alaa, into agreeing to drive me to a checkpoint, where I would turn myself in. Looking back, there was no logic to it, only a desperate hope that I could somehow convince the regime to let me leave. I didn't want to die in Moadamiya; I didn't want to be another body, a number. I may have thought that I could get out of Syria and do something, make a difference from afar, but that is just hindsight. In the moment all I could think of doing was surviving.

My friend Abu Omar would go with me anywhere; Qutaiba and Alaa had different motivations. Qutaiba's elder brother had died in the chemical attack, and he had never really recovered from the loss. He was constantly seeking dangerous situations and would throw himself into any endeavour for his friends, the riskier the better. It wasn't hard to convince him to help me, and Alaa was so close to Qutaiba, he would follow him anywhere. We piled into Abu Omar's car, and he drove us into the night. No one was outside when we arrived at the regime checkpoint; all the guards were inside because of the cold weather. One of them waved at us. Abu Omar parked the car. We looked at each other and got out.

We walked across and entered a large prefabricated cabin with pictures of Bashar al-Assad plastered all over the walls. The television was tuned to the regime's TV station, and a teapot bubbled on a fireplace in the middle of the room. A table covered with cooked chicken and

Arab sweets sat next to the fireplace. At the head of the table two big men sipped vodka. Their guns were across the room, right next to where I was standing.

When we walked in, they smiled and stood up to welcome us, saying their superior officers would be here soon. They walked towards us and extended their hands to shake. We were unsure what to do, but we knew that our lives were at stake and there was no room for error. We shook hands.

We sat down. After a while Qutaiba started mocking the Assad regime's TV broadcasts. I held my breath. My eyes darted back and forth between the soldiers across the room and their AK-47s next to me, but the soldiers just laughed and changed the channel to MBC Action, a satellite channel that broadcasts English-language action movies. The other pushed the sweets in my direction and asked if I wanted one. I knew then that these men were not ordinary *Shabiha*, who would have been aggressive and boastful, throwing their little authority around until their superiors arrived, when they would cower and fall into line. These men were professionals.

Finding safety in strangers
4 February–13 March 2014

Over the next few minutes our *Shabiha* captor-hosts were thoroughly engrossed, or pretended to be, in the movie playing on the television. I maintained a nervous silence. Then two cars slowly pulled up at the checkpoint, and four middle-aged men wearing tracksuit trousers and Adidas jackets climbed out. They came in. The two *Shabiha* stood and saluted. We were not sure what to do, but we felt too frightened by our situation to refrain from showing basic manners. We stood up and said hello.

The men identified themselves as officers in the 4th Division. They told us that they would escort us to the Dama Rose Hotel in Damascus. When we arrived at the hotel, they said, there would be others waiting for us, and everything would be 'taken care of'. They didn't ask us anything about our intentions and were clearly trying to make us feel as comfortable as possible, which was unnerving. Both Qutaiba and Alaa were armed, but the officers didn't seem to care and took little notice as Abu Omar tried to persuade them to leave their weapons behind, in order to show that we were surrendering

and that there should be good will on both sides. Finally
Qutaiba relented, and Alaa followed suit. They placed
their guns on the table and we left with the officers.

Alaa, Qutaiba and two of the officers rode in the first
car, while I, Abu Omar and the two other officers brought
up the rear. We had to pass through five different checkpoints just to reach Damascus, but we weren't stopped; the
checkpoint guards just waved us on. Only two minutes
later we merged on to the Mezze Road, which is the main
thoroughfare in central Damascus. The nighttime crowds
were eating, drinking, laughing and smoking as if nothing was wrong with the world, as if none of their former
neighbours were starving or being tortured to death just a
short distance away.

The next landmark we reached was Umayyad Square,
where the *Sword of Damascus* thrusts towards the sky, a
proud symbol of the city's ability to withstand capture by
the many empires that had risen, then fallen, throughout
its long history. Built in the early 1960s, it was originally
decorated with the flags of the Arab nations as a symbol
of unity and peace. But tonight the *Sword* seemed to be
weeping; raindrops beaded and lingered on its hilt, then
fell to the ground as the *Sword* gently cried them away.
After a few more minutes the cars slowed to a stop in
front of the hotel. An attendant scurried towards us, smiling when he saw the officers' faces.

The Dama Rose had once been home to UN ceasefire
monitors. Now they were long gone, as were most of the
foreign journalists who used to stay there. I had not been
to the Dama Rose since 2009, when I had taken a pretty
blonde flight attendant on a date to the restaurant there
– a rebound from Reem that led nowhere. Though the
building looked the same as before, the hotel guests were

very different. The Syrian politicians and military officers who had once frequented the Dama Rose were gone. In their place, generals with Iranian, Lebanese, Iraqi and Russian accents now milled about in the lobby.

An officer beckoned me towards the elevators, told me that we would have dinner soon, and that I could have a shower and sleep afterwards. Abu Omar was probably as terrified as I was, but he could clearly see my distress and tried to calm me down. Even the officers saw how unnerved I was and tried to cheer me up. I had turned myself in, expecting torture, even death, but here they were booking me into the Dama Rose Hotel.

Two room keys were handed to us. We took the elevator up to the sixth floor then parted to go to our separate rooms. When I opened the door to my room, it was to find three men from Moadamiya waiting inside: Dr Omar and Dr Yazan, who had looked after the few sick Moadamiya civilians in Assad's hospitals, and Hassan Ghandur, an Air Force Intelligence agent who headed Assad's local cease-fire committee. After they had introduced themselves, Hassan suggested we eat before we got into any kind of discussion and led the way to the restaurant, where Abu Omar, Alaa and Qutaiba joined us.

We had a meal unlike any we had eaten in years: grilled chicken, French fries, kebab, hummus, bread, Pepsi. I had forgotten that food like this even existed. I felt like a traitor when I remembered that my friends in Moadamiya were still starving to death, but I could not keep myself from eating. I stuffed bread into my mouth; I slurped down cold fizzy soda; I attacked crispy chicken breasts, eating one after another until I felt sick.

When I had eaten my fill, I recalled what all the civilians who had left Moadamiya during the ceasefire, some to their deaths, had told me before their evacuation: *I would rather die on a full stomach than from hunger.* Now I knew what they meant. I felt ready to die after eating a meal like that.

I was offered a cigarette, and I turned to face Hassan Ghandur as he began to speak.

Hassan told me only to relax and get a good night's sleep. In the morning we would head to 4th Division headquarters and meet General Ghassan Bilal, chief of staff to Maher al-Assad. Alaa and Qutaiba would be staying the night with their families in Damascus, before returning home to Moadamiya the next morning. No one seemed interested in them. We said our goodbyes, and they walked out into the night, while Abu Omar and I returned to our separate rooms.

I could not sleep; I kept waiting for a *Shabiha* to bash in the door, pull me out of bed and drag me into a prison cell. Only after I had said the early-morning prayer and recalled every Quranic verse I knew did sleep finally take me by surprise.

The next day, at around noon, Dr Yazan arrived at my room to escort me to lunch. When we had finished our lunch, Yazan invited me to his room and put away both our cellphones. He suggested a cigarette on the balcony and winked at me. I understood that we were being watched. When we were outside, he spoke freely. Two weeks ago, he had been kidnapped by Air Force Intelligence as he was leaving the hospital in Mezze, and was driven blindfolded to their headquarters at the Mezze airbase when a 4th Division patrol rescued him and returned him to the hotel. He told me not to trust anyone, that I was on my own and needed a plan to escape. He also told me that the Syrians were tired, losing their ideals. They just wanted an end to the violence, and we were seen as troublemakers no one would miss.

We did not visit the 4th Division's headquarters that day, nor on either of the following two days. This gave me many hours to sit in my hotel room and consider Dr Yazan's words. If they wanted me dead, I would already be dead. If they wanted me tortured, I would already be in a cell. They needed me for something. Maybe it was enough for them that I had left Moadamiya – that alone would destroy my reputation among those who remained. Nobody in Moadamiya would ever trust me again; they would be too frightened that I was a regime double agent. The regime knew what they were doing when they let me through the checkpoint.

On the third day Abu Omar left; he needed to return to Moadamiya. Again, no one seemed to care, and we said goodbye not knowing if we would meet again. At noon Hassan Ghandur called to inform me that it was time to visit 4th Division headquarters. They had waited until I was alone. I summoned all my courage and walked downstairs to the main lobby, where Hassan was waiting. When I arrived, Hassan was in the middle of an interview about local ceasefires with two journalists for the *Los Angeles Times*. I did not know the reporters' names, but they somehow knew who I was. Addressing me as Qusai, they asked how I was doing and expressed happiness that I was still alive. Hassan was clearly impressed that the reporters recognized me, while I felt relieved that two American reporters had seen him with me, hoping this meant I would not just disappear without a trace. I tried to extend our encounter for as long as possible, thinking that if I turned up dead, the reporters would remember my face.

We left to drive to the 4th Division and meet General Bilal. Ten minutes passed before we reached the headquarters. They felt like seconds. My mind zoomed through my entire thirty-year life, and I wondered if it was all about to come to a bloody end. It was a beautiful afternoon. The sun beamed her bright orange rays on to the road ahead of us, and a shy, delicate rainbow briefly arched through the sky. As we neared the mountains, the peaks plunged us into shadow. I recited some prayers and Quranic verses, took a deep breath and tossed a roll of chewing tobacco into my mouth.

The guards at the gates performed a brief search before letting us through. Inside the base we passed many soldiers, but something was wrong: most of the soldiers were young and skinny, as if they had only just been recruited from college. Some were not even holding their guns correctly. This was not what I expected from Assad's elite forces. I began to feel more confident. Perhaps Assad's war machine was not as invincible as I had thought.

The car pulled to a stop. An officer towered over me. He was well over six feet tall and looked as if he weighed more than twenty stone, but he had a disarming grin on his face. He was wearing a civilian outfit, jeans and a black leather jacket, and he had a large gun strapped across his back. He told me his name was Yasir Salhab, but I could call him Abu Hassan. He said he was a big fan of my work, that he tuned into Al Arabiya and Al Jazeera every day to hear my voice. He invited me inside his office, offered me tea, coffee, a cigarette.

We entered his office, which was nothing more than a small caravan in the middle of an open area. The caravan contained only cheap leather chairs and an old TV. I was stunned to see that the TV had a satellite receiver, which

would have allowed any intelligence agency in the world
to listen in. As Abu Hassan and I sat down, I noticed
that there were official documents scattered all over the
chairs and floor. I didn't understand this show of amateurism. A ringing telephone announced the start of Round
One. Abu Hassan answered, then asked if he and Hassan
Ghandur could come along to my meeting with General
Bilal. I said yes – what else was there to say?

Soon a well-dressed secretary escorted us to General
Bilal's office.

A small, rich-looking gentleman welcomed me with
a wink. He smiled, then hugged me. Before the revolution I had seen Bilal many times while working at the
hotel. I had shared a powerful friend with him – Abu
Naeem, a casino owner who had later exchanged his life
of luxury for a chance to join the people in their revolution against Bashar al-Assad. But after years of fighting,
I had forgotten what Bilal's face actually looked like. He
was surprisingly ordinary.

He asked me to call him Abu Hamza and said he was
glad to finally meet me. We began our discussion with
forced pleasantries, flattering each other with empty
words. When he told me he was sad that I had said
harsh things about him on the radio, I responded that he
had been harsh in other ways. The men all laughed and
praised my honesty. They told me they respected my love
for Syria.

Abu Hamza asked if I preferred to be addressed as
Qusai or Kassem. When I said he could use whichever he
preferred, since he knew both names, he said he knew me
well, he knew my family and my late father. But he chose
to call me Qusai because that was the hero he wanted
to meet, the man who had so many media contacts.

Now I began to understand what they wanted, why they were treating me so well. They wanted to use me for my Western contacts; they wanted me to act as a mouthpiece for the regime. Abu Hamza praised me further, but when I turned his praise into a question about how our town had come to be gassed, he quickly became less friendly.

I tried to rectify my mistake by asking how I could help them. Abu Hamza told me if I spoke positively about local ceasefires, if I tried to reconcile the so-called rebels with the Syrian *government* – not the regime, the *government*, and if I made sure not to encourage supporters of foreign intervention in our beloved country, I could save thousands of lives. The ceasefires were crucial to the regime, part of their strategy to escape international pressure and shape a false peace process, which would eventually lead to the rebels surrendering. I agreed to help.

They asked me what I needed, and I said I would like time to think. They told me whenever I was ready, Hassan would pass on a message to General Bilal, and if my family needed anything, they would be taken care of. I thanked them and mentioned that it had been a long time since I had seen my family. When they said I should give them my family's contact details, I couldn't believe they thought I was so naive. I took my time responding, then said that unfortunately all of my relatives were out of the country, but perhaps I could get some time off to see my mother. I was thinking ahead, desperately. They ended the meeting with further pleasantries. I had survived round one.

I spent the next few days at the hotel, deep in thought. I was constantly brainstorming various feints, excuses and conversation topics that might buy me more time. After years of starving helplessly under siege, I was not used to sitting comfortably in a hotel room, eating good meals and sleeping without fear of bombardment, but material comforts helped clear my mind and gave me a sense of greater control over my life.

On the third day after I met Bilal, I heard some women screaming outside my door. When I opened the door to investigate, I was set upon by three large men, beaten and kicked, then dragged through the hotel lobby and into a security room, where three men in suits were waiting for me. A 'detective' sat down across the table from me and began interrogating me with profanity-laced questions. I couldn't quite follow what he was saying, but at some point he mentioned the screaming women and demanded that I 'confess' before he called in Air Force Intelligence to take me away.

Try as I might, I could not keep myself from crying when he said that. I felt humiliated, helpless and angry to have been dragged on the floor like a dog and assailed with so many false accusations. I was disoriented and having flashbacks to when I was taken from the falafel shop. The detective picked up his cellphone to make the call. Suddenly I heard the familiar voices of Hassan and Abu Hassan. They were yelling. I recalled Dr Yazan's story – that he was kidnapped, then 'rescued' by a 4th Division patrol. This was all an act. They were trying to weaken me emotionally and make me feel that only the regime could protect me from the regime.

The detective ran for the door, but Hassan, Abu Hassan and a dozen armed men from the 4th Division 'detained' him then feigned deep concern for my well-being. My captors begged Hassan, myself and everyone else in the room for mercy and forgiveness, but Hassan only shook his head and asked me what I thought should be done to the men. But I did not want to play this game. Two attractive women then rushed into the room and started pawing at my arms and legs. I assumed they were the women who had been screaming outside my hotel door earlier. They said they'd do anything I wanted if I would just forgive them. The implication was clear. Again, I said I was not interested. I asked to go back to my room.

We filed paperwork on the incident, and Hassan then took me to a different room in the hotel for my 'protection'. To ensure that I was even safer, he assigned me three armed men as bodyguards supposedly under my personal command. I spent almost an hour in the shower that night, examining the bruises on my legs, arms and torso and wondering how I could have cried like a baby in front of the fake detective when I was supposed to be such a brave revolutionary. I was ashamed.

The next morning I called Bilal and thanked him for his men's help the previous night. I accepted his offer to work for the regime but asked for a favour. I told him I felt bad about what had happened, but it was already on social media and might hit mainstream media soon, so everyone would think I was speaking under duress and wouldn't believe a word I said. Could I go to Beirut for a few days, to meet my family, reassure my media contacts and tell them face to face that I believed in the ceasefires?

Bilal was silent. He was clearly sceptical of the idea. He told me he needed to run it past Maher.

In the ensuing days Hassan Ghandur harassed me with interview requests from pro-Assad media channels and worked doggedly to persuade Bilal not to allow me to leave. I don't know how I managed to fend off Hassan – it was exhausting and took all my focus and concentration – but after a while Bilal must have concluded that I would not give in, because he returned my call. We both

adopted our faux-friendly personas. He told me Maher
had approved my request, but there was one small hitch:
they couldn't get me across the border under my own ID,
so I'd have to acquire a forged one. I was to ask my friends
to create a new ID, give it to them, and they would handle
the security clearances and transportation.

I agreed but said I needed to return to Moadamiya in
order to procure the fake ID from my friends. After two
more days, at around midnight, Abu Omar and I drove
back into Moadamiya. That was one of the worst nights in
my life. I wanted to tell my old friends the truth about my
situation, but I could not explain the game I was playing.
I just couldn't risk sharing my plans with anyone. They
offered me only cold stares, guarded replies and cruel
jokes that mocked me as a traitor. It hurt even more that
these were FSA fighters I had been friendly with only days
before. After about a half-hour the verbal barbs became
too much for me, and I yelled at them before storming off
to walk aimlessly around the town until my feet hurt, in a
vain effort to dull the pain in my heart.

Abu Omar eventually pulled his car alongside me and
told me to get in. I wanted to tell him everything, but
I knew I couldn't. We then spent a few hours driving
through the streets of Moadamiya, touring the remnants
of my old life, until I asked to see my childhood home
one last time.

The apartment was dark. We turned on our cellphones
for light – a truly reckless thing to do – but neither of us
cared about consequences at that point. Abu Omar even
lit a cigarette and began dancing to songs playing on his
iPhone. I sifted through the wreckage of my home one
last time. I was overcome. Everything seemed so special
and precious; every memory seemed fresh. I could see

Mama in the kitchen, my elder brothers Ghilan, Bara
and Razwan getting into stupid fights. I remembered
the football games, the movie nights, the family dinners.
I remembered it all like a sweet dream. I wanted to lie
down on the floor and sleep, but Abu Omar managed to
talk me out of it. Instead I took a few items as mementos
and said goodbye to my home for good.

In the morning I visited three close friends from high
school: Anas, Adel and Ammar. We had been in the same
class, and Adel had lost his father at a young age, just
like me. We had become like family after that, Adel and
I. Both he and Anas had given up studying for their law
degrees to become activists when the revolution began.
Anas took pictures and videos, giving victims a voice and
a memorial; Adel worked in Moadamiya's aid committee,
which ensured that destitute families received the food,
medicine and money that they needed; and Ammar had
been active in the local council before the revolution,
using his influence there to obtain money for the Free
Syrian Army. We had spent the greater part of the siege
together, and it had changed us all irrevocably. Although
I couldn't tell them all the details of what I was going
through, I knew I had to say goodbye.

The four of us had an early breakfast with Turkish
coffee. In case I was killed or disappeared, I had filmed a
video that told the truth about my plans to escape so that
my friends in Moadamiya would know how I had died
and would understand that I had not turned my back
on them. I left this with Anas, who I trusted to keep my
secret and only tell my friends and reporters at the right
time. When we were done with breakfast, I gathered my
belongings and retrieved my real ID, that I had hidden
with a neighbour called Nasser – I knew I would need it.

Then I steeled myself to leave Moadamiya once and for all, but before I left, I received a reminder of my old life.

As part of the ceasefire, civilians were being allowed to return to Moadamiya and check on their homes, or what remained of them. Thousands of residents had streamed into Moadamiya with the sunrise. Among them was Reem, my first love. I spotted her amid a throng of people, accompanied by her mother, near the entrance to the town. She was wearing sunglasses, so I couldn't make out her expression at first, but I imagined that her heart was beating like a war drum inside her chest. When she saw me, she took off her sunglasses and flashed that beautiful smile that I loved. I was expecting my heart to jump through my throat when she smiled. It did not. Instead, although my mind raced through all my memories of her, I felt numb.

We met and exchanged greetings, and then I walked with them as they made their way back to their old home. I couldn't bring myself to ask about her father or her husband, and it was clear that they were nervous and afraid, so I tried to comfort them with some lousy jokes and casual bravado. I don't think I succeeded. Their apartment had been severely damaged by regime shelling, probably because it was on the fourth floor, which made it a prime location for Free Syrian Army snipers. When Reem's mother went inside, she cursed. Reem remained outside with me and stared mournfully at the ruins of her home. I gazed at her beautiful, dejected face as I recalled the dreams that we had shared together. Was it really so long ago that we had had hope? Had so much time passed since we truly believed that we could build a life together?

I remembered knocking on this very door as a teenager, entering this very apartment and asking for Reem's hand in marriage even though I had no money and no job prospects. So much had happened since then. *What would happen to us both?* This last thought drained the strength from my legs and I sat down awkwardly to recover myself. Reem shed a tear, smiled and reached out a hand to help me up, but her outstretched arm only drove a dagger through my heart. As she extended her hand, her wedding ring glinted in the sun. I drew in my breath sharply, stood up before her hand reached my shoulder and faked a smile. We went in, helped her mother pack whatever items she could salvage and smoked a few cigarettes. I called Abu Omar and asked him to give Reem and her mother a lift. When he came, they climbed into his car and drove off, leaving me behind.

By this time, other neighbours and friends were arriving. Their hugs and words of encouragement gave me the strength I needed to get on with my plan, so I called some trusted people who I knew could get me a forged ID. Samer, a friend five years my junior whose family was close to mine, came up with one. I had known him since he was born; he'd been a friend of my younger brothers, and I had come to regard him almost as a brother himself.

Samer had been a hero of the revolution from the start. He had rushed to join the very first protests in Moadamiya, and during the first *Shabiha* massacre in 2012 he was severely wounded by shrapnel when a mortar bomb exploded right next to him. During his recovery he had been shot by *Shabiha* who broke into the apartment he was in. Somehow, miraculously, he had survived, only to suffer through the siege with us. The ID Samer gave me didn't look anything like me. It had belonged to a man who had been visiting a friend in Moadamiya in 2012 when he was killed by a sniper. Because he had died before the Assad regime tightened the siege, he was not on any list. He had also never been reported dead, since no one had been able to locate his family, so his ID card was still active in government records. I took the ID, thanked Samir and finally left Moadamiya for good.

Back at the hotel in Damascus, I presented the ID to Hassan Ghandur, expecting to be allowed to leave for Lebanon within the next day or two. However, Hassan kept changing my departure date and trying to delay my trip. After a couple of days of incredible stress, I decided that I needed to take matters into my own hands. I stopped a taxi, asked to be taken to 4th Division head-quarters along with a friend, and embarked on one of the most mind-blowing car rides of my life. We went through a maze of security checks, talking our way past numbers of suspicious guards, but managed to see Bilal and Abu Hassan to demand that they carry out their end of the bargain. They kept promising that I would leave for Lebanon 'soon', but I kept refusing to leave until we got a promise that 'soon' would be 'tomorrow'. We went back to the hotel. A tense day passed with no news, and I feared the worst. Then, at around noon on the second day, I received a phone call from Bilal.

A few hours later, Hassan arrived to escort me back to 4th Division headquarters. There we sat for hours waiting 'for the car to arrive' while Hassan and Abu Hassan grilled me about my plans for Lebanon. Every few minutes I would make clear that I was only visiting Lebanon to see my family and to reassure my media contacts. I spent a great deal of time listing names and media contacts in the Western press, while trying to reveal as little as possible about my family and making certain to avoid reveal-ing any family member's location. At around 10 p.m.

Bilal called to give us the green light to leave, and my cross-examination was over. His personal car pulled up and we climbed inside and sped off. Hassan and Abu Hassan both said that they would ride with me until I cleared the last regime checkpoint, but that once I arrived in Lebanon, I was on my own.

I had no idea how I could get into Lebanon with the ID of someone who looked nothing like me. I also dreaded what would happen to me if I was unable to make it past the border. As we drove, I asked Hassan and Abu Hassan if they had made any arrangements with the Lebanese authorities. Abu Hassan's reply filled me with terror. He told me they didn't have jurisdiction there; I would have to figure it out myself.

The road to Lebanon was choked with Assad check-points – 4th Division, Air Force Intelligence, Syrian Republican Guard, internal security forces – but we cleared them all with three magic words: 'Master Maher's car'. At one point the driver got bored with the silence and decided to brag about his driving skills. He was in the middle of regaling us with the story of how, a few months ago, he had swerved sharply to avoid an accident while escorting some 'Korean guests' when Abu Hassan rudely cut him off and demanded he change the subject.

I was focused on how I could make my way into Lebanon, but no matter how hard I tried, I could not think of a concrete plan. Eventually I gave up and recited prayers and passages from the Quran under my breath in the hope that God would send me a solution.

After forty-five minutes or so, we reached the Syrian border checkpoint. The driver asked for my ID and the required fee of 1,500 Syrian Pounds, then, without even getting out of the car, yelled to a border guard, handed him the money and the fake ID, and ordered him to process the paperwork as quickly as possible. The guard scurried away. Three minutes later I received the ID back, and we drove through the last regime checkpoint, then stopped. Hassan and Abu Hassan got out of the car to give me a hug. When we had said our goodbyes, they drove away, and I walked towards the Lebanese border alone. It was almost pitch-black. There were no street lights and almost no cars. The few cars I waved at to try and hitch a ride sped past me without stopping.

After about thirty minutes I reached the Lebanese border and joined hundreds of other Syrians waiting to enter. They were being blocked by two Lebanese officers yelling a steady stream of insults and curses. Children cried, women pleaded with the guards, and the old silently bowed their heads as they awaited their chance to bid farewell to their country. I took a personal information card and filled it in. In the 'profession' field I wrote that I was a *New York Times* reporter in the hope that I could pass for one with my English skills, and that the guards would hesitate to abuse an international journalist. One hour later it was my turn. I faked a smile, handed my papers to the border guard and prayed that he would not peer too closely at my photo ID.

The officer took the ID card, bent down to peer at it – a very bad sign – and then looked up at me. But just then, by God's grace, one of his fellow officers yelled out a joke and started laughing. The guard turned to laugh with his friend, turned back to stamp my passport, and shouted, without even looking at me, 'Next!'

I took my documents and walked away. I was incredulous at what had just happened and hurried in case the guard changed his mind. I headed off, trying to hail a taxi, but all of them were full, so I continued on foot. After a full hour I finally boarded a bus. When the bus left I texted my mother on my Syrian cellphone then turned it off, took out the battery and removed the SIM card. I was now off the regime's radar – I hoped. I later dumped the phone and bought a Lebanese one.

Leaving your country during a conflict is probably one of the worst emotional experiences anyone can go through. I was confused, afraid, disappointed, happy I was safe but sad that this might be the last time I would ever see my home. For the next three weeks I found safety with strangers and took great care to avoid old friends. Old friends were dangerous; I could never tell if they had been blackmailed into working for the Assad regime. Most of the people I stayed with in Lebanon were foreign reporters I had known only through Skype. They turned out to be some of the best people I've met in my life, because they cared about me even though they had no reason to.

I continued talking to the media about the situation in Syria and about Assad's crimes. I denounced the local ceasefires, which I saw as tactical moves to escape international pressure to lift the sieges. The ceasefire in Moadamiya forced the rebels to evacuate the town, which eventually happened two years later because the regime kept up its blockade and bombardment even after the ceasefire was declared. I also discussed my hunger strike campaign and described the suffering and civilian casualties that I had witnessed. I even told some personal stories that I had never shared before, such as my near-death experience on Chemical Day. Other incidents I kept to myself, either because I was not ready to share them, or because I did not think any of my media contacts would believe me.

In Lebanon I was stunned by the kindness of people I barely knew. Though I was ashamed to accept so much help, I accepted it none the less, because I craved more than anything the feeling that I had not been abandoned. The kindness I received was a touching reminder that, despite all I had suffered and all the friends I had lost, there was still a lot of good in the world. I experienced simple pleasures from my earlier life that had become almost foreign to me: watching a Barcelona football match, drinking coffee in the morning, smoking a cigarette, eating chocolate . . . I began to feel safe, even without a grenade in my pocket or a gun under my pillow. I stopped hating and fearing dogs; I forgave the dogs-turned-wolves of Moadamiya, which had only gone crazy from hunger like the rest of us. The sound of planes became less alarming to me after I saw some fly overhead without dropping bombs.

I became more vulnerable. Qusai, my fierce fighting persona, started to fade away as the old Kassem returned. I got in touch with my family, mostly through Skype and Facebook. I had been wearing my armour for so long that I was exhausted. I was looking for safety and peace of mind, for a warm hug and some sweet words telling me that everything would be all right. Although I was surrounded by amazing people, this only made me miss the safety I had once felt in Moadamiya even more.

But I needed to find a way out of Lebanon. Syrian-Americans I did not even know had arranged a visa for me to enter the United States, but they had done so under my real name, not under my fake ID. This meant that I needed to find a way to leave Lebanon using my real name, even though there was no record of me having entered the country from Syria. A woman from the

Swedish embassy named Elin – one of the nicest people I have ever met – stepped in to help. She had read my blog while I was on hunger strike and befriended me after I arrived in Lebanon. On the night before I was planning to book my ticket to the United States she threw a party at her boss's house and insisted that I attend. What she neglected to tell me was that the party was in my honour. When I arrived, all of the other guests were strangers to me, but they knew exactly who I was and were eager to help. One woman at the party, named Alia, gave me the following advice: 'The only way out is to turn yourself in to the Lebanese authorities. Get yourself kicked out of the country, because if you try to leave Lebanon through the normal route, they'll never let you. You need to get yourself kicked out of Lebanon, then leave for America on the same day.'

I booked myself a flight to America scheduled to depart at midnight the following evening, and on the morning of my flight walked into Beirut airport to turn myself in. To explain why I had sneaked in from Syria, I said I was a student and had a scholarship in the US, but the Syrian authorities had refused to let me travel because I was a Syrian-Palestinian. The Lebanese official I asked for help unleashed a string of profanities about the negative character traits of Syrians, Palestinians and, worst of all, Syrian-Palestinians, but in the end he bought my story. He told me that I would receive my passport at the airport three hours before my flight and that if I did not leave the country within twenty-four hours, I would be detained and sent back into Syria.

That evening I said goodbye to all my new friends, asked for their prayers and best wishes and headed back to the airport for my flight. Two reporters named Max and Diyaa, who had become good friends during my time in Lebanon, offered to accompany me to ensure that I arrived there safely. They escorted me as far as the security check, which was as far as they could go, before hugging me and bidding me farewell. Having cleared regular airport security, I looked for the booth where I could collect my passport, but when I explained my situation the officer mocked me and said I'd be sent back to Syria.

Inside I flew into a panic; outside I tried to stay calm. I texted every person I could think of to inform them of my situation, then sat down to await my fate. One part of me told me to stay where I was and I would get my passport; another part of me just wanted to dash from the terminal and hide from the police. In the end I suppressed my instinct to flee and sat silently, patiently, reciting every Quranic verse I knew, in the hope that Allah would have mercy and rescue me from my quandary. Phone calls poured in from inside Lebanon and around the world, in both Arabic and English, as my new friends expressed their concern and asked how they could help.

After about thirty minutes, four Lebanese officials approached me. One of them asked if I was Kassem. I said yes. They reassured me that I would get my passport and that they would escort me to the plane.

The phone calls from around the world kept coming in. I told everyone who called me my new situation. Finally an officer arrived, and produced my passport. I made my way to the departure gate and handed it to a boarding agent. She refused to check me in, as my passport only had four months left before it expired. I told her I knew this, my destination country knew too, and I had received my visa just five days ago. She was unmoved. She told me that in order for me to board I needed permission from all of the airports I would pass through – Dulles in the United States and Doha, the transfer airport in Qatar.

I couldn't believe it.

The officials who had helped me before started directing passengers to other desks and remonstrated with the boarding agent, but she refused to budge and called airport security. They arrived and began yelling at the officials. Each side made phone calls to their higher-ups, while I watched and waited to see how Allah would decide my fate. I grew steadily more nervous with each passing minute.

Only ten minutes before my flight was scheduled to depart, I received the permissions that I needed, the flight having been delayed so that I would have time to board. It was my first time flying. I could hardly believe I was in a plane, instead of watching one circle overhead wondering where and when it would drop its bombs. I thought of Majed, my childhood friend who had become one of Assad's fighter pilots. I wondered if he felt this thrill every time his plane lifted off the ground.

I landed in Washington, cleared security and walked outside into the brisk winter air. Everywhere there were Americans. American accents, American flags, American cars, American shops: everything I used to read about back when I was a child looking at my father's *Reader's Digest* magazines.

There was no need to worry about saving food for a siege. There was no need to watch my back for fear of *Shabiha* arresting me. There was no need to show fake respect any more.

I pinched myself a few times to confirm this was not all a dream, smiled broadly and lit a cigarette. I was free. Or was I?

Hope extinguished
March 2014–December 2015

For a long time after I arrived in the United States, I felt like I was daydreaming. A Syrian-American who I knew through a fellow activist picked me up from the airport and took me to his house, where he and his wife fed me turkey and mashed potatoes. We went on a driving tour of Virginia – I was amazed at the lush green fields and open spaces – and we visited downtown Washington, where I saw monuments that I had only seen before on the news. Everything felt so strange – the people, the malls, the trams, the restaurants.

There were only two days between my arrival in America and a weekend of events held in Washington DC to draw attention to the Syrian revolution. At these events I met many Syrian-Americans who had taken time off work and travelled from all over the country to show solidarity with the Syrian people. While I appreciated their efforts, it all felt so remote from the reality of the situation at home, especially during the culminating rally. Protesting didn't seem real without snipers or machine guns firing at the crowd. Only 1,400 people were present, although everyone around me was talking about the massive turn-out, and I noticed that the majority of the protesters were Syrian. This was especially disappointing for me. Where were all the Muslims and non-Syrian Arabs? Why weren't more Palestinians supporting a revolution of the oppressed? And where were the Americans? Didn't they realize Syrians were fighting for the same freedoms that they held dear? I had thought that, since the United States prided itself on its democratic values, the murder of civilians agitating for democracy would make a lot of Americans very angry, but I didn't realize until I reached the US just how ignorant about world events the average American was. During rallies and events near the White House lots of locals asked, 'Where is Syria?' and 'What are chemical weapons?'

The weekend also included two dinners: a fundraiser for humanitarian supplies and a second one to honour Syrian activists. But I could barely eat at either event, even though I was one of those being honoured. I found myself constantly comparing my situation to the grim realities inside Moadamiya. I was homesick, and I felt a terrible sense of guilt because here I was, safe, while millions at home were suffering.

After the events in Washington, I started attending meetings with American policymakers organized by the Syrian-American lobby. I was surprised that a pro-revolution lobby had managed to organize itself in such a short time, especially since many Syrian-Americans risked repri-sals against their relatives at home for speaking out against Assad. It also seemed that the lobby had opened channels to ensure that the plight of the Syrians would reach the highest levels. It appeared there was a real chance of influ-encing government policy. When I first attended these meetings, I had high expectations. I thought, or hoped, that if American policymakers heard from a survivor of Assad's war crimes who could describe in English what he had experienced and witnessed, then US policy would become more sympathetic to our cause.

Some Syrian-American activists also organized a tour for me to speak at universities and other venues across the United States. This tour was extremely difficult for me because all of my experiences still felt so raw. I would get nauseous in the middle of speeches, run to a bathroom to throw up and return to the lectern to resume my talk. While I was speaking, my head would fill with feelings of guilt, homesickness and shame. I knew that I had to speak out. I knew that if I stopped speaking out I could no longer justify my new life to myself. But I also knew that the tour was preventing me from healing; every time I stepped up to the lectern, I reopened old wounds.

I visited dozens of states during my first few months in America. At most of the venues I felt a mixture of surprise and disappointment. On the one hand, I was surprised at how many people had shown up to hear me speak. On the other hand, I was disappointed that the vast major- ity of the attendees were Syrians, even though we went to Harvard, Yale, Princeton and other elite universities where students and staff could be expected to be inter- ested in world affairs. While I appreciated the support of my fellow Syrians, I knew that the chances for US action in Syria were slim unless other Americans began to connect with the Syrian struggle for freedom.

Nevertheless I kept going. I participated in inter- views, connected reporters with activists in Syria and wrote articles about my experiences. I was determined to personalize the conflict. I thought that if I described what

I and my friends had actually experienced, this would inspire ordinary Americans to take up our cause. Despite the frustration and mental pain I felt each time I recalled Assad's atrocities, I made a conscious effort to spread my own story – within the wider story of the Syrian revolution – across the media and within the American government. But I never really felt at home in the United States. Many people were generous to me, and many people were touched by my stories, but at the end of the day I just couldn't get through.

After about a year in the US I had met almost every policymaker who could have made a difference; I had given many speeches and appeared on many news shows in an effort to spread awareness of the suffering of my people, but I had nothing to show for it all and was thinking about returning to Syria. President Obama had made a deal with Iran, a major ally of Assad; Russia had begun assisting the regime with air strikes, and Vladimir Putin had announced his support for Assad to the UN General Assembly. What could I do against such forces? I was pleased when Samantha Power, the American ambassador to the UN, asked me to stand in front of the Security Council as a silent rebuke to those who had voted against sending Syrian war criminals for trial at the International Criminal Court. I was proud at the time I did it, but now I'm not so sure. I wish that, instead of being silent, I had screamed at the top of my lungs.

In December 2015 the Obama administration, working with Russia, initiated the Vienna Diplomatic Process for Syria under the supervision of the newly formed International Syria Support Group. I travelled to New York, where the group's deliberations were taking place. As I sat in the hotel lobby watching diplomats walk by and waiting for them to make their announcement, I had flashbacks to the Dama Rose. The same hollow slogans about peace and negotiated solutions were now being applied to all of the country. Russia and Iran had sent their foreign ministers to mouth empty words about peace while their jets and tanks imposed the law of the jungle on Syria. The end result of these meetings was UN Security Council Resolution 2254, which called for a ceasefire and political settlement but without any mention of account-ability for war crimes. I lost a lot of faith at that moment.

The talks in New York were barely under way when the regime launched a new offensive against Moadamiya and effectively ended the local ceasefire – such as it was. Assad's forces re-blocked the roads into Moadamiya and bombarded the town fiercely, while the Russian military provided new tanks to push through our defences and minesweepers to negate the work of Abu Adnan and all those who had died planting anti-tank devices. My friends in the FSA heard their attackers speaking Farsi over their radios, which meant the Iranian Revolutionary Guard was also involved. Assad's forces also mounted a major chemical attack around this time that some doctors on the scene believe utilized sarin. While the diplomats in New York talked, seven of my friends in Moadamiya died in this offensive.

When I told people that I wanted to go back to Syria, they said I was crazy. Why, they asked, would I want to return to a war zone that millions had fled? They also urged me not to give up on the US. They told me I had post-traumatic stress disorder and advised me to see a psychiatrist. They told me I had a bright future ahead of me in which I would publish a book and attend univer-sity. They bombarded me with text messages urging me to stay. But I was not interested; America was starting to feel too much like a gilded cage. On the morning of 21 April 2016 I boarded a plane bound for Turkey.

The next five weeks could hardly have been more different and more depressing than what I had hoped for. When I left the United States my plan was to cross the Syrian–Turkish border and make my way to Syria's main northern city of Aleppo, but many logistical problems emerged after I left the US, and I was forced to abandon this idea. Instead, I got stuck in the limbo that has afflicted so many Syrian refugees who are now trying to cope with life outside their homeland.

I found my way to Germany, where I applied for political asylum as a Syrian refugee in May 2016.

Epilogue
June 2017

I am now a refugee three times over: born a Palestinian refugee in Syria, displaced from my Syrian homeland alongside millions of others, only to become a refugee again after I left the United States to try and return to my country.

Refugees are now a nation unto themselves. We have no land, no flag and no government (although we do have our own Olympic team), but if we were to coalesce, we would form a nation larger than France or the United Kingdom. So before you blame or judge us all, try to understand who we are and why we've become refugees. Try to imagine yourself living life in our shoes for just one day.

I am concluding this book in July 2017. I wish I could say that by this time the war in Syria had ended or was nearing an end. As I write, it is estimated that nearly 500,000 people have died since the revolution began. Of course the opposition says there are more dead, the regime says fewer. The UN in 2016 said it was close to 400,000. Whatever the true figure, every one of those people meant something, and had a life once, in Syria. Recently, a fact-finding mission by the Organisation for the Prohibition of Chemical Weapons, an inter-governmental organisation located in the Netherlands, concluded that sarin had been used in an attack in April 2017 that killed dozens of people in Khan Shaykhun in northern Syria. But what good is this conclusion now?

In Germany I am trying to piece together a life. Like so many others, I left Syria to build a new life. Did I abandon my country? Do I want to go back? And Syria is in ruins. Will it be rebuilt? How will it be rebuilt? Who will rebuild it?

I don't have any answers. All I can do is pray, and hope, and dream, and remember Syria, my country.

Acknowledgements

Thank you all for helping me when I needed you.

To my beautiful sweet mother who raised eleven children after my dear father passed away, your bravery and sacrifice will forever be a shining light to guide my path.

To my dear father in heaven, your words of wisdom, endless love and hard work taught me how to be a man.

To my beloved brothers and sister, thank you for protecting me, teaching me how to play football, and kicking my ass when I did stupid things.

To my one and only Nicoleta, that night in Berlin changed my life forever, we met in our worst days, but our love made us believe again in life, and I'll never stop believing.

To my dear brother Shlomo Bolts, I could never have written this memoir without your help, I hope one day you'll get the appreciation you deserve for all the hard work you've done to help the people of Syria, I want you to remember that you have my appreciation and love forever.

To Alexandra, Janine, Angelique, and the rest of the amazing Bloomsbury team: thank you for giving me the chance to share my story with the world, thank you for your professionalism, dedication and kindness.

To Mahmoud Sawan, Kenan Rahmani, Alou Hatem, Mouawya Hamoud, Ammar, Anas, Adel, Hakam, Abu Omar, Alam Dar, Abu Adnan, Dr Homam, Dr Fayez, Dr Ali, Dr Abd, Abu Ali, Omar Hossino, Mohammad Ghanem, Bayan Khatib, Rasha Othman, Lina, Salwa, Leen, Lina Sergie, Alia Mansour, Jerry Maher, Elin Hagerlid, Erica, Mohja, Ahmad Churbaji, Zekay Hamoui, Alex, Terry, Andy, Karim, Leon, Maysam, Michelle Ajami, Muna Jondy, Mouaz Moustafa, Nada, Raed Faris, Hadi Al Abdullah, Chad, Khulood, Dr Zaher and everyone who let me sleep on their couch, share their meal, and fought to help the people of Syria, I shall be forever grateful for your love and support. You are my backbone and inspiration, thank you for being who you are.

To Peer, Lauren, Diaa, Max, Anne, Mary, Ruth, Michael, Tom, Loveday, M Ghannam, Arwa, Raja, Hwayda, Louise, Katie, Nicole, Scott, Firas, Rima, Ghada, Hassina, Christy, Christian, Brooke, SE and all the brave journalists who gave me the chance to tell the truth about Syria while the world was trying to hide it.

To Adnan, Jabal, Razan, Tal, Omran, Aylan, Hamzeh, Harmoush, Abdul Qader, James Foley, to every man, woman and child who suffered, to all the martyrs, prisoners and victims of Syria and the world who fought tyranny, dictators and terrorists and gave their lives for freedom, justice, peace and democracy: until the sun rises from the West, until the mountains turn into dust: I will never give up, I will keep fighting, screaming, writing for you until my last breath and heartbeat.

To my country, my everything, my endless love, my Syria.

A Note on the Type

The text of this book is set Adobe Garamond. It is one of several versions of Garamond based on the designs of Claude Garamond. It is thought that Garamond based his font on Bembo, cut in 1495 by Francesco Griffo in collaboration with the Italian printer Aldus Manutius. Garamond types were first used in books printed in Paris around 1532. Many of the present-day versions of this type are based on the *Typi Academiae* of Jean Jannon cut in Sedan in 1615.

Claude Garamond was born in Paris in 1480. He learned how to cut type from his father and by the age of fifteen he was able to fashion steel punches the size of a pica with great precision. At the age of sixty he was commissioned by King Francis I to design a Greek alphabet, and for this he was given the honourable title of royal type founder. He died in 1561.